# EASY ENGLISH

## Basic Grammar and Usage

Diana Bonet

**Crisp Publications, Inc.**
**Menlo Park, CA**

# EASY ENGLISH
## Basic Grammar and Usage

Diana Bonet

## CREDITS

Editor: **Elaine Brett**

Designer: **Interface Studio**

Typesetter: **Interface Studio**

Cover Art: **Barbara Ravizza**

Copyright ©1993 by Crisp Publications, Inc.
Printed in the United States of America by Bawden Printing, Inc.

The Frank and Ernest cartoon by Bob Thaves on the cover of this book has been reprinted by permission of NEA, Inc.

http://www.crisp-pub.com

**Library of Congress Cataloging-in-Publication Data**

Bonet, Diana.
  Easy English : basic grammar and usage / by Diana Bonet.
      p.    cm.
    ISBN 1-56052-198-8 (pbk.)
    1. English language—Textbooks for foreign speakers.  2. English language—Grammar.    I. Title.
  PE1128.B625    1993
  428.2'4—dc20
                                                                    92 – 74206
                                                                         CIP

Crisp Publications, Inc.
1200 Hamilton Court
Menlo Park, CA 94025

This book is printed on recyclable paper with soy ink.

# Preface

English is an amazing language. It is flexible and expressive, and it is a powerful friend when it is used correctly. The better we use it, the better our chances for social and professional advancement. The following pages offer some fundamental grammar and usage rules that really can make a difference in the way we communicate. Perhaps correct spelling and proper pronouns will not increase our savings accounts or build our biceps, but they do give us that measure of skill and self-confidence that make life just a little easier. That's not bad for a colorful little book that has only 170 pages, weighs about a pound, and costs less than two tickets to a first-run movie.

*Diana Bonet*

Diana Bonet

I respectfully dedicate this book to my Hewlett-Packard spring quarter Business English class. I taught them writing and grammar, and they taught me laughter, persistence, and meaningful values.

| | |
|---|---|
| Ada Archibald | Elisa Martinez |
| Julie Barron | Al Meneses |
| Shirley Bentsen | Armando Miclat |
| Roger Carlson | Jenny Nguyen |
| Joe Cuneo | Kim Nguyen |
| Richard Dotson | Maria Quinonez |
| Claudia Florang | Lender Surrency |
| Lang Lee | Betty Tahmasbi |
| Rosalie Maciel | Priscilla Vigil |
| | Julie Walias |

# CONTENTS

PREFACE . . . . . . . . . . . . . . . . . . . . . . . . . . . . . . . . . . . . . . . . . . . . . . . . . . . . i

INTRODUCTION . . . . . . . . . . . . . . . . . . . . . . . . . . . . . . . . . . . . . . . . . . . . v

YOUR GRAMMAR GOALS . . . . . . . . . . . . . . . . . . . . . . . . . . . . . . . . . vii

**CHAPTER I REVISITING THE PARTS OF SPEECH**
Revisiting the Parts of Speech . . . . . . . . . . . . . . . . . . . . . . . . . . . . . .   1
Tripping Through Nountown . . . . . . . . . . . . . . . . . . . . . . . . . . . . .   2
Using Nouns Effectively . . . . . . . . . . . . . . . . . . . . . . . . . . . . . . . . .   6
Pronoun Pass . . . . . . . . . . . . . . . . . . . . . . . . . . . . . . . . . . . . . . . . . .  12
Using Pronouns Effectively . . . . . . . . . . . . . . . . . . . . . . . . . . . . . .  12
Action in Verbville . . . . . . . . . . . . . . . . . . . . . . . . . . . . . . . . . . . . .  17
Using Verbs Effectively . . . . . . . . . . . . . . . . . . . . . . . . . . . . . . . . .  26
Adjective Avenue . . . . . . . . . . . . . . . . . . . . . . . . . . . . . . . . . . . . . .  40
Using Adjectives Effectively . . . . . . . . . . . . . . . . . . . . . . . . . . . . .  46
Adverb Alley . . . . . . . . . . . . . . . . . . . . . . . . . . . . . . . . . . . . . . . . . .  49
Using Adverbs Effectively . . . . . . . . . . . . . . . . . . . . . . . . . . . . . . .  51
Preposition Place . . . . . . . . . . . . . . . . . . . . . . . . . . . . . . . . . . . . . .  54
Using Prepositions Effectively . . . . . . . . . . . . . . . . . . . . . . . . . . . .  56
Conjunction Junction . . . . . . . . . . . . . . . . . . . . . . . . . . . . . . . . . . .  60
Answers to Section I Exercises . . . . . . . . . . . . . . . . . . . . . . . . . . . .  68

**CHAPTER II SENTENCE SENSE**
Sentence Sense . . . . . . . . . . . . . . . . . . . . . . . . . . . . . . . . . . . . . . . . .  79
Four Kinds of Sentences . . . . . . . . . . . . . . . . . . . . . . . . . . . . . . . . .  83
A Brief Pause for the Phrase and the Clause . . . . . . . . . . . . . . . . .  84
"Which, and That—Which Is Correct?" . . . . . . . . . . . . . . . . . . . .  91
About Complete Sentences . . . . . . . . . . . . . . . . . . . . . . . . . . . . . . .  92
Sentence Bits and Pieces . . . . . . . . . . . . . . . . . . . . . . . . . . . . . . . . .  94
Parallel Sentences . . . . . . . . . . . . . . . . . . . . . . . . . . . . . . . . . . . . . .  97
Answers to Section II Exercises . . . . . . . . . . . . . . . . . . . . . . . . . . . .  99

**CHAPTER III USING WORDS EFFECTIVELY**
Using Words Effectively . . . . . . . . . . . . . . . . . . . . . . . . . . . . . . . . . 107
Tricky Words . . . . . . . . . . . . . . . . . . . . . . . . . . . . . . . . . . . . . . . . . . 107
Tacky Words . . . . . . . . . . . . . . . . . . . . . . . . . . . . . . . . . . . . . . . . . . 111
Sticky Words . . . . . . . . . . . . . . . . . . . . . . . . . . . . . . . . . . . . . . . . . . 118
Wacky Words . . . . . . . . . . . . . . . . . . . . . . . . . . . . . . . . . . . . . . . . . . 122
Answers to Section III Exercises . . . . . . . . . . . . . . . . . . . . . . . . . . . 124

## CHAPTER IV SPELLING, PUNCTUATION, AND CAPITALIZATION

Laffing at Misspelled Words . . . . . . . . . . . . . . . . . . . . . . . . . . . . . . .129
Punctuation? Of Course! . . . . . . . . . . . . . . . . . . . . . . . . . . . . . . . . .131
Punctuation That Ends All . . . . . . . . . . . . . . . . . . . . . . . . . . . . . . . . .132
Don't Be a Comma-Kazi . . . . . . . . . . . . . . . . . . . . . . . . . . . . . . . . . .135
What, More Comma Rules? Yes, a Few . . . . . . . . . . . . . . . . . . . . . .145
Are You Semiconscious About Semicolons? . . . . . . . . . . . . . . . . . .147
Uppercase-A Capital Idea . . . . . . . . . . . . . . . . . . . . . . . . . . . . . . . .149
Answers to Section IV Exercises . . . . . . . . . . . . . . . . . . . . . . . . . . .157

## CHAPTER V COMMUNICATING WITH CONFIDENCE

Communicating With Confidence . . . . . . . . . . . . . . . . . . . . . . . . . . .165
Developing a Personal Action Plan . . . . . . . . . . . . . . . . . . . . . . . . .166
Your Personal Action Plan . . . . . . . . . . . . . . . . . . . . . . . . . . . . . . . .167

# Introduction

What made you choose this book? Do any of the following reasons apply to you? I love grammar. I want to improve my writing and speaking in order to impress my (boss, parents, sweetheart, instructor). It's time to "bite the bullet" and learn what I missed in school. I need a quick review. Grammar is important. I am *really* bored. Almost any reason for studying English grammar is a good reason, except perhaps boredom.

English grammar is the way our language puts words together to create sentences. Usage is the study of what is correct and incorrect, according to the guidelines of Standard English. Learning grammar and usage does not have to be painful, or dull. *Easy English* helps you make sense of the language. Even though grammar seems to be full of rules, not to mention the exceptions hidden in the fine print, it can be fun, once you get the hang of it. This book is a practical guide, written with humor and compassion for those who don't like silly rules. In it you will find lots of examples and practice exercises that provide exact answers to your grammar questions.

If you are a student, you will find the practical help that you need to pass your courses and move into the business world with ease. If English is your second language, the sections on usage and articles (*a*, *an*, and *the*) are helpful. Administrative assistants and support personnel will find guidance through the land mine of subject-verb agreement and punctuation. Perhaps you are an employee working toward a promotion and you want to improve your communication skills in speaking and writing. *Easy English* contains chapters on usage, grammar, punctuation, and spelling to help you meet your goals.

If you are wondering whether you are using your time effectively by reviewing the basics of grammar, the answer is a definite "Yes"! A review is an investment in yourself. You want to succeed, and the correct use of English will help you. Think of the last time you hurried to finish a memo or a letter. In your rush you neglected to proofread your document for spelling, punctuation, and typing errors. Really now, could a small oversight make a difference to anyone but the pickiest reader?

Always think twice about giving up accuracy for speed. Whether we like it or not, most readers notice even little mistakes. Don't you? Readers often make quick and lasting judgments that can hurt us permanently without our knowing it, and in ways that we may never realize. Similarly, untidy verbal pronunciation, poor enunciation (lazy lips), and incorrect grammar create negative impressions.

Ignorance is *not* bliss. These errors indicate to listeners that we lack interest in quality communiction. They also suggest a sloppy attitude that reflects on individuals—and the companies they represent. Unconscious or careless mistakes confine many intelligent people to lower-paying jobs with less opportunity for career advancement. Whether we like it or not, an unspoken consensus exists among educated people regarding proper and improper grammar. Small mistakes create doubts about our information and about us as communicators.

In the 1990s and beyond, language and communication skills will be more important than ever. Yes, we need technical knowledge, but we must be able to *communicate* that knowledge. We influence others positively when we can explain our ideas in clear, easy-to-understand language. We add to our credibility when we use words correctly and concisely.

You are reading this book because you care enough to make more informed choices about grammar. You want to recognize errors and correct them. Once you pinpoint a habitual grammar mistake you can practice correct usage. We cannot guarantee that workbook exercises will change a lifetime of grammar errors, nor will correct practice help you write a perfect business letter. However, the exercises in this book provide clear explanations of basic grammar rules; they provide an opportunity to use them correctly, and they present a clear choice between good and poor grammar. Approach the task with a positive attitude, put your heart into your work, and *never* give up!

# Your Grammar Goals

Goals give you purpose and direction. They define what you want to achieve and provide satisfaction when you have achieved them. On the list below, check the goals that are important to you.

☐ Learn to spell words that have been problems for me.

☐ Learn the definitions and uses of the parts of speech.

☐ Apply the rules of grammar to my speaking and writing.

☐ Write clear, complete sentences.

☐ Avoid nonstandard slang and cliches, by golly.

☐ Catch myself in the act of speaking and writing well.

☐ Develop the habit of looking up grammar and usage rules.

☐ Create a plan for continued improvement.

☐ Others

_____

_____

_____

_____

# Chapter *I*

# Revisiting the Parts of Speech

# Revisiting the Parts of Speech

> *"English usage is sometimes more than your taste, judgment, and education. Sometimes it's sheer luck, like getting across the street."*
> —E.B. White

Why should I learn the parts of speech? Check those that apply.

☐ To review grammar, because it is good for me. (So is broccoli.)

☐ To impress my rich Aunt _____ (insert name).

☐ To write error-free sentences.

☐ To discuss the language intelligently.

☐ To express ideas precisely.

☐ To learn other languages.

☐ To distinguish a preposition from a pot-hole.

☐ To understand the foundation and structure of English.

☐ To speak and write correctly when necessary.

☐ To get good grades in school.

English is a reasonably logical language—except for its spelling, of course. All of the words in the English language can be divided into eight categories, called parts of speech: **nouns**, **pronouns**, **verbs**, **adjectives**, **adverbs**, **prepositions**, **conjunctions**, and **interjections**. Every word in English performs one of five functions: it names, expresses action or being, modifies, connects, or expresses emotion. Many words can be used as several parts of speech. A word is classified as one part of speech or another depending on its job in the sentence.

The wild *storm* descended. (Storm is a noun.)

Must you *storm* about the room? (Storm is a verb.)

*Storm* clouds blackened the horizon. (Storm is an adjective.)

Think of this section of the book as a journey. Following is a review of the parts of speech and rules to help you use them. Imagine that each part of speech is a town on a map. Stop at each town and study its rules. These rules will guide you through the basics of English, the elements of the language that you need to know. Are you ready?

# Tripping Through Nountown

> *"Good grammar requires knowledge and skill. It is not for sissies."*
> —Diana Bonet

**Nouns** come in two varieties: **common** and **proper**. **Common nouns** name ordinary people (golfers), ordinary places (banks), and ordinary things (monsters). "Things" can be not only monsters or rocks or trees, but also abstract ideas such as emotions (outrage), ideas (whims), or wishes (solitude), and in some cases, actions (guzzling).

| | |
|---|---|
| People | Nothing motivates **employees** more than seeing the **boss** working. |
| Places | On her way **home** from **work**, Theresa stopped at the **bakery**. |
| Things | Rosita felt **perspiration** trickle down her **nose** as the **sun** grew hotter. |
| Ideas | The **secret** to **happiness** is to find your own **truth** and to live it. |
| Feelings | Bob's **emotions** soared as he felt the **joy** and the **fear** of **winning** the lottery. |
| Actions | The **giggling** stopped and the **growling** and **complaining** began. |

**Articles** (*a*, *an*, and *the*) introduce nouns. That is, they tell you that a noun is about to appear. Sometimes a word or two may come between an article and its noun (*a* corny joke) (*an* old shoe) (*the* very ripe tomato).

Try this test for a noun: Mongo is puzzled about the (his) _____. Some words that you write in the blank may sound silly, but if they make sense they are likely to be nouns.

## ■ EXERCISE FOR PRACTICE

Circle the common nouns in the list below. You should find 10 nouns in the list. Check your answers at the end of this section.

| | | | |
|---|---|---|---|
| soft | astronaut | ask | cabbage |
| yet | miserable | locker | under |
| Wow! | owl | growled | coward |
| dull | nerd | feebly | not |
| trucker | college | workbench | dragon |

**Proper nouns** are always capitalized. They name *specific* persons, places, or things. *Note:* First words in a sentence are also always capitalized, but don't assume that they are always proper nouns. Acronyms (such as ID for identity) are also not necessarily proper nouns.

My boss, **Tangles McQuade,** reports to **Su Hong** in the **Marketing Division**.

The water stain on the lobby carpet in **Building Twelve** is shaped like **Alaska**.

**Elvis** drank **Pepsi**.

## ■ EXERCISE FOR PRACTICE

Underline the proper nouns in the sentences below. The number of proper nouns in each sentence is shown in parentheses. Two capitalized words in a name are considered one proper noun. Check your answers at the end of this section.

Examples:  Levi immigrated from Bavaria and worked in New York until last June. (4)

Dr. Sung reported that Jupiter is twelve times larger than Earth. (3)

1.  I was born in Australia because my mother wanted me to be near her. (1)

2.  Despina watches history being made on CNN. (2)

3.  The Human Resources Department offers accent reduction classes in English, Spanish, and Japanese. (4)

## ■ EXERCISE FOR PRACTICE

In the following exercise, underline each common noun and capitalize each proper noun. The number of common nouns and proper nouns in each sentence is indicated in parentheses at the end of the sentence. Check your answers at the end of this section.

Examples:     B̸asil, ɣ́ri, and ǿlaf signed a <u>petition</u> for higher <u>wages</u>. (2 common, 3 proper)

            <u>Visitors</u> filled the <u>hallway</u> and <u>lobby</u> to see the new Ẃackdobit. (3 common, 1 proper)

1. Otis stays in his office and fills out forms instead of visiting his engineers in peoria. (3 common nouns, 2 proper nouns)

2. On monday, visitors from india and taiwan are inspecting our new orleans assembly plant. (2 common nouns, 4 proper nouns)

3. Acme designs spends one million dollars in research and development between january and june. (3 common nouns, 3 proper nouns)

4. Katherine krump keeps one-eyed bats, helpless kittens, and other stray creatures in her kitchen on staten island. (4 common nouns, 2 proper nouns)

5. Most of our executives drive toyotas and hondas. (1 common noun, 2 proper nouns)

# Who Said English is Easy?

We'll begin with a box; the plural is boxes,

But the plural of ox is oxen, not oxes.

One fowl is a goose, but two are called geese,

Yet the plural of mouse should never be meese.

You'll find a lone mouse, or a nest full of mice,

But the plural of house is houses, not hice.

If I speak of a foot, you show me your feet

And I give you a boot, would a pair be called beet?

If one is a tooth, and a set is called teeth,

Why wouldn't the plural of both be called beeth?

If the singular's this, and the plural is these,

Should the plural of kiss be written as keese?

One may be that, and two would be those,

Yet hat in the plural would never be hose.

And the plural of cat would never be cose.

We speak of a brother, and also of brethren,

But though we say mother, we never say methren.

The masculine pronouns are he, his, and him,

But imagine the feminine, she, shis, and shim!

English is funny; on that we agree,

But alphabet soup makes no sense to me.

Author Unknown

# Using Nouns Effectively

> *"When I make a mistake, it's a beaut!"*
>
> —Fiorello LaGuardia

To use nouns effectively, you must follow a few rules. These rules govern changes from singular nouns to plural forms: mouse to mice; house to houses (not *hice*). And they dictate the way that nouns show ownership: boss to boss'; wolf to wolves'. Because the words in our language came from so many sources, nouns change form often. Please don't take this personally. These changes allow us to express ideas easily, with color and drama. Stay close and step lightly. Learning to use nouns and to master their spelling will build your confidence quickly and it will enhance your usage skills.

## SINGULARS AND PLURALS

A noun is **singular** when it refers to one person, place, thing, or idea.

| | | | |
|---|---|---|---|
| geek | rainbow | flower | crewcut |
| hundred | opera | assembler | secret |
| nut | manager | telephone | Ted |

A noun is **plural** when it refers to more than one person, place, thing, or idea. Nouns usually form plurals by adding *s* to the end of the word.

| | | | |
|---|---|---|---|
| geeks | rainbows | flowers | crewcuts |
| hundreds | operas | assemblers | secrets |
| nuts | managers | telephones | Teds |

Nouns that end in *ch, s, sh, x,* and *z* require an *e* before the plural *s*. Otherwise the plural form of the noun would be difficult to pronounce.

| | |
|---|---|
| one church | two churches (not churchs) |
| one fax | two faxes |
| one mess | two messes |

If a noun ends in a consonant (any letter of the alphabet except *a, e, i, o, u*), followed by a *y,* the plural is formed by changing *y* to *i* and adding *es.*

| | | | |
|---|---|---|---|
| company | companies | sky | skies |
| family | families | buggy | buggies |

**NOTE:** If a vowel comes immediately before the final *y,* simply add an *s* to form the plural.

| | | | |
|---|---|---|---|
| donkey | donkeys | day | days |
| turkey | turkeys | boy | boys |

Plurals of most nouns ending in *fe* or *f* are formed by changing *f* to *v* and adding *s* or *es.*

| | | | |
|---|---|---|---|
| one knife | two knives | one scarf | two scarves |
| one life | two lives | one wolf | two wolves |

**NOTE:** Just to confuse you, some words ending in *f* and *fe* don't follow their own rules. *Roof, proof, safe, chief,* and *belief* form the plural by adding *s.* The plurals are *roofs, proofs, safes, chiefs,* and *beliefs.* I apologize for the perverse behavior of these plurals. Some nouns, on the other hand, don't change form when they become plural.

| | | | |
|---|---|---|---|
| one sheep | two sheep | one fish | two fish |
| one moose | two moose | one deer | two deer |

The following words look like plurals but they are used as singular nouns. No one knows why: *news, politics, thanks, savings, physics, billiards, premises, economics.*

## COLLECTIVE NOUNS

A *collective noun* names people, ideas, or things as groups.

| | | | |
|---|---|---|---|
| team | jury | class | Friends of Starving Students |
| U.S. Senate | association | committee | flock |

Although collective nouns refer to groups of people or things, they are considered singular nouns because we think of them as a unit.

## PERPLEXING PLURALS

Some nouns have tricky plurals that do not follow the rules. Many of these words came from Greek and Latin. Some words, such as *scissors* and *measles*, have no singular form; others have two plural forms: *appendices, appendixes*. Here is a list of singular nouns and their irregular plurals. To use these singular and plural nouns effectively, become familiar with this list and learn to spell each correctly.

| Singular | Plural | Singular | Plural |
|----------|--------|----------|--------|
| alumnus | alumni | ox | oxen |
| child | children | potato | potatoes |
| crisis | crises | quiz | quizzes |
| datum | data | self | selves |
| elf | elves | thief | thieves |
| foot | feet | thesis | theses |
| goose | geese | tooth | teeth |
| hero | heroes | wife | wives |
| index | indices | woman | women |
| leaf | leaves | yourself | yourselves |
| louse | lice | | |

## ■ EXERCISE FOR PRACTICE

The dictionary is a great resource for uncovering plural forms of nouns. Use your favorite dictionary to look up the plurals of the following words and write them on the lines next to the singular form. If you can't find a dictionary, guess the answers, then check them at the end of this section.

Examples:  forty ___forties___       series ___series___

crisis ___crises___       mouse ___mice___

1. brother-in-law _____      5. handful _____

2. cactus _____      6. zero _____

3. life _____      7. measles _____

4. ox _____      8. fungus _____

## ■ EXERCISE FOR PRACTICE

Decide whether each of the following nouns is singular or plural. Write **S** or **P** beside the number. If it is both singular and plural, write **BOTH**. If the noun is singular, write the plural form on the right; if the noun is plural, write the singular form on the right. Check your answers at the end of this section.

Examples:    __BOTH__    sheep    __sheep__

             __S__    valley    __valleys__

             __P__    calves    __calf__

1. ___ children _____

2. ___ fleece _____

3. ___ Smith _____

4. ___ lady _____

5. ___ peas _____

6. ___ secretary _____

7. ___ comedy _____

8. ___ oxen _____

9. ___ coats _____

10. ___ goose _____

11. ___ mother-in-law _____

12. ___ thousand _____

13. ___ box _____

14. ___ scarves _____

## POSSESSIVES

When one noun names a thing that belongs to another noun (dog's biscuit), use an apostrophe (') to show ownership.

### Singular Possessives

To form the **possessive** of a singular noun, simply add an apostrophe and an *s*.

the computer's keyboard  =  the keyboard belonging to the computer

a baby's smile        =  the smile belonging to the baby

the goon's balloon     =  the balloon belonging to the goon

If the singular noun already ends in *s*, or other hissing sounds, don't worry. To make the noun possessive, add an *'s*.

| | |
|---|---|
| Professor Bones's lecture | = the lecture belonging to Professor Bones |
| the boss's decision | = the decision belonging to the boss |
| the class's reunion | = the reunion belonging to the class |

**NOTE:** You probably noticed that it seems awkward to have three *s*'s on the end of a word. For this reason, some intelligent people now drop the final *s* on singular nouns that already end in *s*, especially for proper names: St. James' Place, Dickens' novels. The final *s* is dropped because language becomes simpler as it evolves. However, other equally intelligent people insist that the old rule still applies. A reasonable guideline would be to drop the final *s* on singular nouns ending in *s*, especially for proper names, when your writing is informal – for example, in internal letters and memos. If you are writing formal documents such as term papers, scientific studies, or research reports, stick to the old rule. Then you will never be wrong.

### ■ EXERCISE FOR PRACTICE

On the lines provided, write the possessive of each of the following singular nouns. Check your answers at the end of this section.

Examples:   fox ____fox's____          girl ____girl's____

goodness __goodness'__          Mr. White __Mr. White's__

1. goddess _____          6. Mr. Jones _____

2. moose _____          7. hero _____

3. copier _____          8. story _____

4. employee _____          9. pension _____

5. dress _____          10. Bess _____

**Plural Possessives**

If a plural noun ends in *s* (boys), simply add an apostrophe to make it possessive (boys').

governesses' duties                    ships' captains

countries' flags                       employees' rights

If a plural noun does not end in *s* (geese), add an *'s* to make it plural possessive (geese's)

children's toys                        fish's gills

women's issues                         mice's tails

When a noun is both plural and possessive, think of the plural form first, and the possessive form second. Compare these four forms of *city*.

| | |
|---|---|
| **Singular** | the city |
| **Singular and possessive** | the city's government |
| **Plural** | the cities |
| **Plural and possessive** | the cities' governments |

## ■ EXERCISE FOR PRACTICE

Write the possessive form of the following plural nouns in the spaces provided. Check your answers at the end of this section.

1. churches _____

2. customers _____

3. sheep _____

4. savings _____

5. classes _____

6. warranties _____

7. unions _____

8. feet _____

9. reports _____

10. Joneses _____

## Pronoun Pass

> *"Make every word pay its own way."*
>
> Strunk and White

A **pronoun** is a word used in place of a noun. Pronouns are handy because we don't have to repeat words. Without pronouns we would be forced to say the silliest things:

> *Chivley's manager told Chivley that Chivley must watch Chivley's expenses closely.*

Using pronouns, we can change this absurd sentence to a shorter, less absurd sentence:

> *Chivley's manager told him that he must watch his expenses closely.*

When a pronoun replaces a word or a group of words, the word being replaced is called an **antecedent**.

> Lenny wrote a letter to his *supplier, who* responded quickly. (*Supplier* is the antecedent of the pronoun *who.*)

When you use a pronoun after an antecedent, be sure that the reference is clear.

> George and Lenny went to *his* work station. (Whose work station?)
> Tonya told her boss that *she* needed a vacation. (Who needed a vacation?)

## Using Pronouns Effectively

> *"I personally believe we developed language because of our deep need to complain."*
>
> Lily Tomlin

If a pronoun's antecedent is singular, the pronoun must be singular. If the pronoun's antecedent is plural, the pronoun must be plural. Readers get a little crazed when pronouns and antecedents don't agree.

Our customers want quality and service; *it* must be our first concern. (Oops! *Quality* and *service* are two nouns, so the pronoun must be plural. . . . *they* must be our first concern.)

*One* of the students lost *their* parking sticker. (Oops again. *One* is singular, so the pronoun must be singular. . . . lost *her* parking sticker.)

Here is a helpful list of singular and plural pronouns.

| | |
|---|---|
| Singular only | another, each, either, neither, every, anyone, anybody |
| Plural only | both, all, many, several |
| Singular and plural | some, such, any, some |
| Singulars changed to plurals | one, ones; other, others |

*None* is both singular and plural, but it is most often used with a plural.

### ■ EXERCISE FOR PRACTICE

Underline the pronoun that agrees with its antecedent in the following sentences. Check your answers at the end of this section.

Examples:  Each of the attorneys spent an hour outlining (**her**, **their**) case.

One must decide early in life what values (**he**, **they**) will uphold.

1. Narrow thinkers like Magwich seldom capture the whole truth with (**his, their**) generalizations.
2. The Guard Dog Committee has made (**its, their**) recommendations.
3. Neither Tisha nor Tilly could find (**their, her**) fishing license.
4. Every one of the computers has been shipped to (**its, their**) destination.
5. Both Jason and Samson thought (**their, his**) bosses were terrific.
6. Boyd studied economics because (**it, they**) had always been of interest to him.

## Kinds of Pronouns

Here are some popular pronouns divided into convenient categories. Don't be shocked by the big words that identify the categories. They are harmless, and they help you identify the proper use for each pronoun.

**Demonstrative pronouns** point out words or ideas.
this (these), that (those)

**Indefinite pronouns** address nothing or no one in particular.
all, another, any, anyone, anything, both, each, either, everybody, everyone, neither, nobody, none, nothing, no one, one, some, someone, something, such, and else (when used with another indefinite pronoun, as in *someone else*)

**Interrogative pronouns** ask questions.
who, what, which, whom, whose, whoever, whatever, whichever

**Personal pronouns** show who is speaking, who is spoken to, or who is spoken about.
I, you, he, she, it(s), we, you, they, my, mine, your(s), his, her(s), our(s), their(s), me, him, us, them

**Relative pronouns** relate to an antecedent and introduce clauses.
who, whom, which, what, that (sometimes *as* and *but*)

**Adjective pronouns** are used like adjectives to modify nouns and other pronouns. Some of the pronouns listed above are used as adjective pronouns. Sometimes they are called **pronominal adjectives**.

Demonstratives: this, that, these, those
Interrogatives and relatives: which, that
All indefinite pronouns except *none*.

Examples: *this* ogre *these* ogres *that* critic *some* sharks

## ■ EXERCISE FOR PRACTICE

Underline the pronouns in each sentence. The number of pronouns in each sentence is noted in parentheses at the end of the sentence. Check your answers at the end of this section.

Examples: Make <u>someone</u> happy today—mind <u>your</u> own business. (2)

<u>Those</u> <u>who</u> think <u>they</u> know <u>it</u> all upset <u>those</u> of <u>us</u> <u>who</u> do. (7)

<u>She</u> sold <u>her</u> advertising agency by <u>herself</u>. (3)

1. I am certain that you can be sure of only one thing: nothing is certain. (4)
2. Would you like for me to check the expiration on your access card? (3)
3. I must tell Mr. Binkely that I am quitting and I'm not sure that I have the courage to tell him. (6)
4. Some of my problems were given to me; the rest I created myself. (5)
5. Mamma, this is my friend Mia. (2)
6. I don't know if anyone will remember me after six years. (3)
7. Everyone is entitled to his or her opinion. (3)
8. I'm no different from anybody else who has two arms, two legs, and forty-two hundred hits. *Pete Rose* (3)
9. Our company allows everyone the freedom to be creative. (2)
10. We used a slide projector to show our management team our new product ideas. (3)

## The Case for Pronouns

When deciding what pronoun to use, you need to know how it will be used in your sentence. Will it be a subject or an object, or will it be used to show ownership?

Subject: *She* made donut holes.

Object: Give a donut hole to *her*.

Possession: This donut hole is *hers*.

Pronouns are divided into three categories called **cases**: **nominative, objective,** and **possessive**.

|  | Subject Nominative Case | Object Objective Case | Possession Possessive Case |
|---|---|---|---|
| **Singular** | I | me | my, mine |
|  | you | you | your(s) |
|  | he | him | his |
|  | she | her | her(s) |
|  | it | it | its |
|  | who | whom | whose |
| **Plural** | we | us | our(s) |
|  | they | them | their(s) |
|  | you | you | your(s) |
|  | who | whom | whose |

The **nominative case** of the pronoun is especially for subjects of sentences.

*I* need advice.

*She* is hard to ignore.

*Who* is *she*? (Trust me on this one. *She* is an objective complement. After all, the sentence wouldn't sound right if it said, "*Who* is *her*?")

The **objective case** of the pronoun is for any kind of object, except, of course, the object of your affection. It is used for a direct object, an indirect object, or the object of a preposition.

| | |
|---|---|
| Direct object | Remember *me*? |
| Indirect object | The committee gave Bozo and *her* a special award. |
| Object of a preposition | To *whom* do you wish to speak? |

The **possessive case** of the pronoun shows ownership.

These are *her* flippers.

Is this coffee *yours*?

*Their* cars are in *our* parking spaces.

**NOTE:** The possessive form of the pronoun does not use an apostrophe: *its, hers, yours, ours,* with the exception of *one (one's* own).

### ■ EXERCISE FOR PRACTICE

For more practice, underline the correct pronouns in each of the following sentences. Check your answers at the end of this section.

Examples: The army will present (**its,** their) colors at the parade.

There are those (**who,** whom) don't even like to be rubbed the right way.

Neither Bacchus nor Sigfreid knows (**his,** their) Social Security number.

1. It was (**I,** me) who wrote the blistering memo.
2. No one deserved the Bellyflop Award more than (**he,** him).
3. The information was given to (we, **us**) in confidence.
4. The safety training class begins (**its,** their) first session today.
5. Neither Raoul nor Gomez can decide what (**he,** they) wants for (**his,** their) birthday.

6. The jury reached (**its, their**) verdict quickly.

7. Tom Wu wants to know (**who, whom**) is in charge of the maintenance shop.

8. The Excellence in Action certificates were awarded to Janet and to (**he, him**).

9. Nothing is mysterious about (**I, me**), except that nobody knows (**who, whom**) I am, where I came from, or why I am here.

10. The Sales Department's oompah band presents (**its, their**) first concert on Friday.

## Action in Verbville

> *Verbs may be tense and moody, but don't assume you can shift their tenses and moods whenever the whim seizes you.*
> Karen Elizabeth Gordon

The verb is the heartbeat of the sentence. It tells you what's happening. The verb is the engine that moves the subject to act, or to be something. It asserts something about the subject. Even if a sentence contains only one word, that word must be a verb: Scat! Whoa! (Every sentence must have a subject, whether it is spoken or merely understood. In sentences such as *Scat!* and *Whoa!* the subject is implied; it is the word *you*.)

The bull *snorted*.

Percy *waved* to the crowd.

Tran *is* eager to begin.

(You) *Hold* it!

*Verb test:* Insert a suspected verb into this sentence. It must be singular and in the present tense (time). I _____ **it**. If your word makes sense, it is a verb.

### ■ EXERCISE FOR PRACTICE

Fill in the blanks with your own verbs to complete the following sentences.

Examples:  Gumby __thinks__ too much.

Marcello __blinks__ at his manager.

At the end of the month Winston __spends__ his money.

1. Helmut _____ English, but he _____ math.

2. If the order comes tomorrow, will you _____ it?

3. Nadia _____ when she is promoted.

4. She _____ the Big Bad Wolf, so it _____ her.

5. The robot _____ and _____, but I _____.

*FRANK & ERNEST reprinted by permission of NEA, Inc.*

## TYPES OF VERBS

Verbs are classified according to the presence or absence of complements, also called **direct objects**. Do not confuse complements with compliments.

> **Complement:** Sadie drank the *prune juice.*

*Prune juice* is the complement that completes the information presented by the subject and verb. It tells you *what* Sadie drank.

> **Compliment:** You look so young!

This compliment is pleasant flattery, unless of course you are trying to look older.

### Transitive Verbs

Verbs may be **transitive** or **intransitive**. A verb is transitive when it requires a **complement** (a **direct object**) to complete its meaning. A direct object can be only a noun or a pronoun, and it receives the action of the verb.

> Quimby *craves* mashed potato *sandwiches.*

*Sandwiches* is the direct object and it receives the action of the verb *craves*. Therefore, *craves* is a transitive verb.

An easy way to look for a direct object is to ask *who* or *what* after the verb.

Craves *who* or *what*? *Sandwiches.*

(*Mashed potato* tells what kind of sandwiches.)

If a sentence answers the *who* or *what* question, it has a direct object and the verb is **transitive**.

### ■ EXERCISE FOR PRACTICE

Underline the transitive verbs in the sentences below. Circle the direct objects of the transitive verbs. Check your answers at the end of this section.

Examples:   Ming gained (confidence) as he worked.

The training program outlines our (objectives.)

My parents warned (me) about people like me.

1. Delbert unloaded the delivery truck.
2. Our manager supports the TQM program.
3. The security guard changed the lock.
4. Suki left her shoes in the mailbox.
5. Forgive me.

### Intransitive Verbs

An **intransitive verb** does not need a receiver (a direct object or complement) to complete its meaning. There are two kinds of intransitive verbs. One is an action that is complete by itself. This kind of intransitive verb is often followed by a prepositional phrase, as in this sentence:

Spotty barked *at the mailperson.*

**NOTE:** A prepositional phrase does not answer the *who* or *what* question directly. If we say, "Spotty licked the mailperson," the verb is transitive because *mailperson* is now the direct object. The direct object answers the question "Licked whom?"

The other kind of intransitive verb is a linking verb. Linking verbs do not show action. They simply link the subject to a word in the predicate (verb part of the sentence).

Michael *is* sincere.

### ■ EXERCISE FOR PRACTICE

Underline the intransitive verbs in the following sentences. Check your answers at the end of this section.

Examples:   Our work group <u>argued</u> about the project.

I never <u>travel</u> without my diary.

Supplies <u>are</u> limited. (*Limited* is an adjective, so it is not a direct object. *Are* is a linking verb.)

1. Paulo cheered wildly.
2. I was twenty on January 20.
3. Sit down.
4. Claribelle went to Transylvania for a vacation.
5. The secretaries gossiped about the strange new receptionist.
6. Life is nice; it is something to do.
7. Sales improved over the fourth quarter.
8. All employees are responsible for good telephone manners.
9. We have been working all morning.
10. Your manager will be Mrs. Fibley.

**NOTE:** Some verbs are always transitive (*ignore*), some are always intransitive (*seem*), and some can go either way, depending on their use in the sentence. The labels *v.t.* and *v.i.* in your dictionary tell you whether or not a particular verb requires a direct object.

### Active and Passive Verbs

Verbs can also be classified as active or passive. When the subject *performs* the action, we say the verb is **active**. When the subject *receives* the action of the verb, we say the verb is **passive**. Active verbs are important in business writing because they are easier to read; sentences are shorter and less cluttered when verbs are active. Use passive verbs sparingly when you write.

## Active Verbs

The following sentence contains an active verb:

Oaks *grow* in the meadow.

*Oaks* is the subject, and *grow* is the verb that tells you what the oaks do, or what action the oaks perform. *Grow* is an active verb.

### OTHER EXAMPLES

Bainbreath *sent* the fax. *Bainbreath* is the subject of the sentence. He is the one performing the action: *sent*.

Jules *studied* for the exam until midnight. The verb is active because Jules (the subject of the sentence) is the one who performed the action: *studied*.

## Passive Verbs

*The test was given by the lab assistant*. This is an example of a sentence with a **passive verb**. *Test* is the subject, and *was given* is the passive verb. When the verb is passive, the subject is being acted upon. The verb *was given* tells you what was done to the test.

### OTHER EXAMPLES

The puppy *has been given* a bath.

Mr. Bigley *was asked* about the fire code.

A kind heart *is* not *recommended* in the game of chess.

### ■ EXERCISE FOR PRACTICE

Indicate a **P** for a passive verb or an **A** for an active verb for each sentence below. When you have finished, go through the sentences again and write **T** for transitive or **I** for intransitive at the end of each sentence. Check your answers at the end of this section.

Examples:  __A__  Some people really eat brussel sprouts.  __T__

__A__  Our organization supports recycling.  __T__

__P__  The cat was killed by curiosity.  __I__

__P__  The contract has been cancelled.  __I__

1. \_\_\_\_ You will be asked for a donation. \_\_\_\_

2. \_\_\_\_ Both of us cannot behave irrationally at the same time. \_\_\_\_

3. \_\_\_\_ An Indonesian guest will tour our testing laboratory this afternoon. \_\_\_\_

4. \_\_\_\_ Suki left. \_\_\_\_

5. \_\_\_\_ Farquar might be allowed at the table. \_\_\_\_

6. \_\_\_\_ The proposal was rejected by management. \_\_\_\_

7. \_\_\_\_ Billbob's group focuses on teamwork. \_\_\_\_

8. \_\_\_\_ Regis lives near the junkyard. \_\_\_\_

9. \_\_\_\_ We humans must make a cruel choice: work or daytime TV. \_\_\_\_

10. \_\_\_\_ Gilda will be promoted. \_\_\_\_

## Linking Verbs

Yet another way to classify verbs is *action* versus *state of being*.

> Stonewall *is* sensitive.

*Stonewall* is the subject and *is* is the **linking verb**. This verb does not describe action, because no action is happening. Linking verbs are always non-action words. The linking verb is telling you something about Stonewall's condition. It links *Stonewall* and *sensitive*. You can use an equals sign to determine whether a verb is a linking verb: Stonewall = sensitive.

The word *sensitive* is called a **complement**—a word that renames or describes the subject. Linking verbs are also called **state of being verbs**. They are forms of the verb *to be*. Following is a list of linking verbs:

> be, am, are, is, was, were, being, been

Sometimes two linking verbs are used together to form a **verb phrase**.

> I *will be* president.

Linking verbs are also verbs of the senses, such as: *feel, look, hear, taste, smell, sound*. Other linking verbs include: *seem, remain, appear, become*. These verbs can sometimes be action verbs as well as linking verbs. Here are some examples:

To feel:

I *feel* lightheaded after riding the Tonsil-Tilt. (*feel* is a linking verb)

Did you *feel* the quality of the wool cloth? (*feel* is an action verb)

To remain:

I *remain* your lovable friend. (linking)

Toby *remained* at the office, even though his boss had left. (active)

To sound:

The Blue Notes *sound* terrific tonight. (linking)

*Sound* the alarm when the lights go out. (active)

Examples of linking verbs:

The cabin *seems* cozy.    *Cozy* describes the cabin. *Seems* is the word that links *cabin* and *cozy*.

Jose *is* a fan of MTV.    *Jose* and *fan* are the same. *Is* is the linking verb.

## ■ EXERCISE FOR PRACTICE

Underline the linking verbs in the following sentences. Check your answers at the end of this section.

Examples:   You <u>are</u> the best!

The computer <u>looks</u> new.

Quimbe <u>will be</u> the treasurer.

1. That building was our research division.

2. A bird in the hand is too small for dinner.

3. Rhonda has been our tax expert for years.

4. The engineers were fans of ''Star Trek.''

5. Apples taste good.

6. This bid will be our final offer.

7. The twins seem identical.

8. Rosebud feels sick.

9. The tired employees are cranky.

10. One seventh of our lives is spent on Mondays.

## Auxiliary Verbs

**Auxiliary verbs**, sometimes called **helping verbs**, join with action verbs to show the tense, or time of an action.

Regis *is living* near the junkyard.

*Living* is the active verb, and *is* is the auxiliary verb. The active verb and the auxiliary verb form a **verb phrase**. Following is a list of auxiliary verbs. (You have already seen some of these words in the list of linking verbs.) They are forms of the verb *to be*:

am, are, is, was, were, be, been

Other auxiliary verbs that you might see as parts of a verb phrase include:

have, has, had, do, does, did, may, might, must, can, could, shall, will, should, would

Some auxiliary verbs can also be main verbs:

I *did think* of you while you were away. (auxiliary)

Flaubert *did* his chores with relish. (main verb)

Poor drivers *have hit* this curb before. (auxiliary)

Poor drivers *have* problems with this curb. (main verb)

In the following sentence, the verb phrase contains four words.

Mr. Chang *will have been working* since 5:00 a.m.

The words *will have been* are auxiliary verbs. *Working* is the active verb. The complete verb phrase is *will have been working*.

## OTHER EXAMPLES

We *ought to be leaving*.

Pancho *has been riding* horses for six months.

I *must sell* my pet boa constrictor.

The company *might be asked* for a donation.

## ■ EXERCISE FOR PRACTICE

In the following exercise, underline the complete verb phrase. Check your answers at the end of this section.

Examples:  The guppy <u>is swimming</u> upside-down.

Our group <u>was leading</u> in the contest.

The cyborg's department <u>has been releasing</u> the parts too slowly.

1.  Heraldo should receive the reward.
2.  Jeeves will show you to the door.
3.  Mrs. Turtletaub has given me another assignment.
4.  A stitch in time would have confused Einstein.
5.  Our secretary will be routing the memo through electronic mail.
6.  We have told him everything.
7.  The auditors will be completing their work on time.
8.  The committee is serving garlic ice cream.
9.  The furnace has been behaving strangely.
10. Our accountant has issued new tax forms.

# Using Verbs Effectively

> *Hard writing makes easy reading.*
>
> —Unknown

## SUBJECT-VERB AGREEMENT

Subjects and verbs must do their best to agree with each other. If the subject is singular, the verb must be singular; if the subject is plural, the verb must be plural. What's wrong with the following sentence?

Alejandro show his etchings to anyone who are interested.

If you said the verb should be *shows*, you are correct. *Shows* is a singular verb and it must agree with *Alejandro*, who is a singular subject. Also, *anyone* is singular so the verb *are* must also be singular (*is*). The sentence should be: Alejandro shows his etchings to anyone who is interested.

Choose the correct verb in the following sentence.

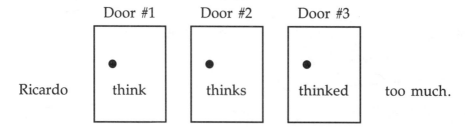

Ricardo [Door #1: think] [Door #2: thinks] [Door #3: thinked] too much.

If you said Door #2, you win. (Please do not hold your breath until your prize arrives.)

Singular:

Ralphie *seems* tense.

Music *calms* the savage beastie.

Our company *is* Cycle Cybernetics.

The health plan *was* ridiculous.

Plural:

Ralphie and Letty *seem* tense.

Savage beasties *calm* themselves with music.

Our companies *are* Cycle Cybernetics and the Recycle Cycle Shop.

The health plans *were* ridiculous.

### Something Has Come Between Us

Subject-verb agreement is usually simple, except for a few teensy exceptions:

**Modifiers sometimes intrude between the subject and its verb.**

*Lights* on the printer *tells* you when to add paper.

This sentence is incorrect because *lights* is the subject and it is plural; therefore the verb must be *tell* (plural), rather than *tells* (singular), in order to agree with the subject. *Lights* ~~on the printer~~ *tell* you when to add paper.

Don't be led astray by words that come between the subject and the verb. Always make the verb agree with its subject. To avoid confusion, cross out prepositional phrases between the subject and the verb and then see what the verb should be. Objects of prepositions sometimes look like the subject, but they are only toying with you. Objects of prepositions never occur as subjects.

NOT: Some people in the department *has* the flu.

YES: Some people ~~in the department~~ *have* the flu.

NOT: The leaves of the gocha-gocha tree *is* poisonous.

YES: The leaves ~~of the gocha-gocha tree~~ *are* poisonous.

NOT: Ricardo, along with Maria and Chrissy, *were* late for class.

YES: Ricardo, ~~along with Maria and Chrissy~~, *was* late for class.

**In sentences where subjects follow verbs, be especially careful to find the real subject and make it agree with the verb.**

Along *come* Jones, with his banjo on his knee.

*Jones* is a singular subject, therefore the singular verb should be *comes*, to agree with the singular subject.

In some sentences writers reverse the usual word order to achieve a dramatic or surprising effect. Generally, you should avoid this style because it is difficult to read; and of course, the subjects and verbs play hide-and-seek with the reader.

**In sentences that begin with** *Here, There,* **or** *Where* **followed by forms of the verb** *be,* **the subject follows the verb.**

WRONG: Here *is* the invoices that were lost.

*Invoices* is the subject and it is plural, therefore the verb should be *are*, which is plural, to agree with the plural subject. Here *are* the invoices that were lost.

NOT: There *is* two secrets to staying young: avoid stress and lie about your age.

YES: There *are* two secrets to staying young: avoid stress and lie about your age.

NOT: At the end of the hall *is* several empty conference rooms.

YES: At the end of the hall *are* several empty conference rooms.

**In questions, the verb (or part of it) comes before its subject.**

WRONG: *Has* Terrance and Amanda *seen* your new office?

*Terrance* and *Amanda* are plural subjects, therefore the verb should be *have seen*, which is plural, to agree with the subjects. *Have* Terrance and Amanda *seen* your new office?

NOT: *Is* all of you ready for the audit?

YES: *Are* all of you ready for the audit?

NOT: *Was* any of them spelunkers?

YES: *Were* any of them spelunkers?

## ■ EXERCISE FOR PRACTICE

In the following sentences underline the subject; then circle the verb choice that agrees in person and number with the subject. Check your answers at the end of this section.

Examples:   Several <u>members</u> of the staff (**give**, gives) to charity.

There (is, **are**) too many <u>programmers</u> working on the project.

Why (is, **are**) <u>you</u> and <u>I</u> the only ones here?

1. The surest way to remain a winner (**is, are**) to win once, and then not play any more. *Ashleigh Brilliant*

2. Angel, as well as Simon, (**want, wants**) all of the power and none of the responsibility.

3. From the mouths of babes (**come, comes**) eternal truth.

4. People who do their best even when they don't feel like it (**are, is**) called professionals.

5. Out of nowhere (**step, steps**) my hero.

6. There (**is, are**) too little time to finish the project.

## GETTING TENSE WITH VERBS

Kitty drove the bumper car tomorrow.

She will fly the hang glider yesterday.

Don't these sentences make your hair hurt? You can tell instantly that something is wrong, which shows that you already know something about **verb tenses**. *Tense* comes from the Latin word *tempus*, meaning *time*. Verbs tell us not only *what* action is occurring, but also *when* it is occurring. The sentences above had their own time built in. The past tense *drove* told you that Kitty had already run her errand with the bumper car, and that's why the word *tomorrow* tweaked your brain. Also, *will fly* indicates the future and seems out of place with *yesterday*.

To express tense, verbs change form or combine with other verbs. There are six tenses: the **present**, the **past**, the **future**, the **present perfect**, the **past perfect**, and the **future perfect**. The two main forms are the **present** and the **past tense**. The past tense is usually formed by adding *-ed* to the basic verb.

| Present | Past |
|---------|------|
| help | helped |
| glide | glided |
| mutter | muttered |
| telephone | telephoned |
| prove | proved |
| ask | asked |

Verbs that follow this pattern are called **regular verbs**. Thanks to the French influence on the English language, most of the verbs in English are regular. However, 100 or so verbs from the original Old English remained in the language, and they do not follow the regular form. These are known as **irregular verbs**. (In Old English they were known as ''strong verbs.'') They are listed later in this section on pages 34-36.

Only the past and present tenses are expressed in single words (change, changed). The other tenses require certain auxiliary verbs (helping verbs) to indicate changes in time. In the future tense, the auxiliary verb *will* expresses future time.

| Past | Present | Future |
|------|---------|--------|
| jived | jive | will jive |
| insulted | insult | will insult |

## Present Tense

The **present tense** of the verb indicates that an action or a condition is occurring now, or that it occurs regularly.

Vincent *yawns* during Economics class.

I *am* for the metric system, every inch of the way.

Diego *likes* the software package.

## Past Tense

The **past tense** of the verb indicates that an action or a condition is completed.

Vincent *yawned* during Economics class.

I *was* for the metric system, every inch of the way.

Diego *liked* the software package.

## Future Tense

The **future tense** indicates an action or a condition that will take place. To express the future tense, the auxiliary verb *will* is used.

Vincent *will yawn* during Economics class.

I *will be* for the metric system, every inch of the way.

Diego *will like* the software package.

## ■ EXERCISE FOR PRACTICE

In each sentence below, change the verb to the tense indicated at the end of the sentence. Write the verbs on the lines at the left. Check your answers at the end of this section.

Examples:    __will see__    I *saw* the movie. (future)

          __needed__    Ernest *needs* the report. (past)

          __exceeds__    The new product line *exceeded* our expectations. (present)

1. _____ Betty Crocker *uses* a mix. (past)

2. _____ Emile *refused* to accept telephone calls during the conference. (present)

3. _____ The committee *recommended* a payroll access code. (future)

4. _____ We will *recover* our losses at the end of the quarter. (past)

5. _____ Toothaches *tend* to occur on Saturday nights. (future)

6. _____ The instructor *required* two copies of the term paper. (present)

7. _____ I *need* a break. (future)

8. _____ Kimiko's soup *will contain* lentils, chipped Spam, celery, and alfalfa. (past)

9. \_\_\_\_ Too much technical vocabulary *will hinder* good communication. (present)

10. \_\_\_\_ I *need* help in admitting that I need help. (future)

## The ''Perfect'' Tenses

Don't be concerned about this group of verb tenses. They aren't really perfect, or at least they aren't flawless. *Perfect* is a grammar term indicating that an action has been completed (perfected). There are three perfect tenses: the **present perfect**, the **past perfect**, and the **future perfect**. The perfect tenses express more subtle variations in time. They describe how an event in the past, present, or future continues to completion. The present perfect and past perfect tenses are formed by adding *has, have,* or *had* to the past participle (the *-ed* form of an action verb). The future perfect is formed by adding *will have* to the main verb.

**Present Perfect.** An action occurred in the past and is now complete. You form the present perfect by adding *have* or *has* to the main verb.

Isaac *has completed* his project.

The three contractors *have asked* us for a bid.

**Past Perfect.** An action occurred in the past *before* another action in the past. You form the past perfect by adding *had* to the main verb.

We *had worked* for three hours when help arrived.

I wish that I *had ignored* the fortune cookie.

**Future Perfect.** An action will be completed in the future before another future action. You form the future perfect by adding *will have* to the main verb.

When you arrive Jimbo *will have left.*

I *will have made* six trips to the printer before noon.

## ■ EXERCISE FOR PRACTICE

On each line at the left write the form of the verb requested in parentheses. Check your answers at the end of this section.

Examples:  <u>will have started</u>  Life (start/future perfect) after breakfast.

<u>have asked</u>  I (ask/present perfect) my boss for a chance to prove that money can't make me happy.

<u>had guessed</u>  The students (guess/past perfect) the answers to the study questions.

1._____ Over the winter Zoltan (learn/past perfect) to ice skate, ski and snowmobile.

2._____ You (inspire/present perfect) me to learn to spell *hors d'oeuvres*.

3._____ By next year our start-up company (earn/future perfect) one million dollars.

4._____ The engineers (design/present perfect) a better mousetrap.

5._____ If you roll sixes again, you (roll/future perfect) them five times in a row.

6._____ Within two weeks, Hans (acquire/past perfect) three new clients.

7._____ Economists (guess/present perfect) as accurately as anyone else.

8._____ Bucko (forgot/past perfect) to attend the memory improvement seminar.

9._____ For two years I (listen/present perfect) to the sound of my hair turning grey.

10._____ Throughout the year the employees (cross-train/past perfect) in order to learn new skills.

## IRREGULAR VERBS

Most of the verbs we have used—ask, roll, learn—are called regular verbs because they cooperate nicely, and they form the past tense simply by adding *-ed* to the present (roll, rolled). The past participle of these forms, the form that follows the verb *have* in phrases such as *have stalked*, is the same form as the past tense. The past participle is used to form the perfect tenses.

**Irregular verbs** are those whose past tense and past participle are not formed merely by adding *-ed*. Irregular verbs form the past tense in strange and wonderful ways, which defy even the experts. Therefore, you must study and learn them through practice. If you wish to achieve instant improvement in grammar, begin by focusing on irregular verbs, as incorrect use of irregular verbs causes many embarrassing errors in speaking and writing.

The most commonly used irregular verbs are listed on the chart below. Review this list to find the ones that cause you the most trouble.

## MAIN PARTS OF COMMONLY USED IRREGULAR VERBS

| Present Tense | Past Tense | Past Participle |
| --- | --- | --- |
| am | was | been |
| arise | arose | arisen |
| awake | awoke, awaked | awakened |
| bear | bore | born |
| beat | beat | beaten |
| become | became | become |
| begin | began | begun |
| bite | bit | bitten |
| bleed | bled | bled |
| blow | blew | blown |
| break | broke | broken |
| bring | brought | brought |
| build | built | built |
| burst | burst | burst |
| choose | chose | chosen |
| cling | clung | clung |
| come | came | come |
| dig | dug | dug |
| dive | dived, dove | dived |
| do | did | done |
| draw | drew | drawn |
| dream | dreamed, dreamt | dreamed, dreamt |
| drink | drank | drunk |

| Present Tense | Past Tense | Past Participle |
| --- | --- | --- |
| drive | drove | driven |
| drown | drowned | drowned |
| eat | ate | eaten |
| fall | fell | fallen |
| flow | flowed | flowed |
| fly | flew | flown |
| forget | forgot | forgotten |
| forgive | forgave | forgiven |
| freeze | froze | frozen |
| get | got | got, gotten |
| give | gave | given |
| go | went | gone |
| grow | grew | grown |
| hang (a picture) | hung | hung |
| hang (a person) | hanged | hanged |
| hear | heard | heard |
| hide | hid | hidden |
| hit | hit | hit |
| hurt | hurt | hurt |
| know | knew | known |
| lay (to place) | laid | laid |
| lead | led | led |
| lend | lent | lent |
| lie (to recline) | lay | lain |
| lie (to tell a fib) | lied | lied |
| light | lighted, lit | lighted, lit |
| meet | met | met |
| mistake | mistook | mistaken |
| prove | proved | proved, proven |
| put | put | put |
| read | read | read |

| **Present Tense** | **Past Tense** | **Past Participle** |
|---|---|---|
| ride | rode | ridden |
| rise | rose | risen |
| run | ran | run |
| say | said (not *says*) | said |
| see | saw | seen |
| set | set | set |
| sew | sewed | sewed, sewn |
| shake | shook | shaken |
| shine | shone | shone |
| show | showed | showed, shown |
| shrink | shrank | shrunk |
| sing | sang | sung |
| sit | sat | sat |
| sleep | slept | slept |
| speak | spoke | spoken |
| spend | spent | spent |
| steal | stole | stolen |
| sting | stung | stung |
| strike | struck | struck |
| swear | swore | sworn |
| swim | swam | swum |
| swing | swung | swung |
| take | took | taken |
| teach | taught | taught |
| tear | tore | torn |
| tell | told | told |
| throw | threw | thrown |
| wake | waked, woke | waked, woken |
| write | wrote | written |

### Tense Errors to Avoid

**Do not mistake the past participle for the past tense.**

    NOT:    Suzanna *come* from Alabama.

    YES:    Suzanna *came* from Alabama.

    NOT:    Honey, I *shrunk* the kids.

    YES:    Honey, I *shrank* the kids.

    NOT:    Twitty *run* twenty copies of the agenda.

    YES:    Twitty *ran* twenty copies of the agenda.

**Do not add regular endings to irregular verbs.** This is where ''baby talk'' comes from.

    NOT:    A bee *stinged* me.

    YES:    A bee *stung* me.

    NOT:    Yutzy *throwed* his back out of joint.

    YES:    Yutzy *threw* his back out of joint.

**Do not use present tense for past tense.**

    NOT:    Last night Wilbur *sees* the same rerun on two channels.

    YES:    Last night Wilbur *saw* the same rerun on two channels.

    NOT:    On Tuesday I *says* to my boss, ''I'm working too much overtime.''

    YES:    On Tuesday I *said* to my boss, ''I'm working too much overtime.''

    NOT:    Last week, Suki *finds* her lost pocket calculator.

    YES:    Last week, Suki *found* her lost pocket calculator.

**Do not use the present tense in place of the future tense.**

    NOT:    Tomorrow James *drives* to the distribution center.

    YES:    Tomorrow James *will drive* to the distribution center.

NOT:   Next week I *go* to a convention in Boston.

YES:   Next week I *am going* to a convention in Boston.

NOT:   In a few days I *come* to a decision on my career.

YES:   In a few days I *will come* to a decision on my career.

**Do not use past tense when you mean the past perfect.** This poor rule is so abused!

NOT:   Samantha asked if I *got* what was coming to me.

YES:   Samantha asked if I *had gotten* what was coming to me.

NOT:   I *wrote* my paper by Tuesday.

YES:   I *had written* my paper by Tuesday.

NOT:   Sometime between nightfall and sunrise, Beastilla *drank* the magic potion.

YES:   Sometime between nightfall and sunrise, Beastilla *had drunk* the magic potion.

**Do not confuse the past tense with the past participle.** Only the past participle uses an auxiliary verb.

NOT:   The storm *had blew* over.

YES:   The storm *had blown* over.

NOT:   The telephone *has rang* all morning.

YES:   The telephone *has rung* all morning.

NOT:   Snively *has hid* from reality, but he keeps in touch by modem.

YES:   Snively *has hidden* from reality, but he keeps in touch by modem.

**Do not confuse similar verbs. Two sets of verbs that cause trouble are** *sit* **and** *set* **and** *lie* **and** *lay.*

| Present | Past | Past Participle | "ing" Form |
|---------|------|-----------------|------------|
| sit (to be seated) | sat | had sat | sitting |
| set (to place) | set | had set | setting |
| lie (to rest) | lay | had lain | lying |
| lay (to place) | laid | had laid | laying |

*Set* and *lay* always need an object. *Lie* and *sit* ride alone.

NOT:   The president *was setting* at the conference table.

YES:   The president *was sitting* at the conference table.

NOT:   Talullah *sat* the file on the desk.

YES:   Talullah *set* the file on the desk.

NOT:   *Lay* down for awhile.

YES:   *Lie* down for awhile.

NOT:   The report *is laying* on your desk.

YES:   The report *is lying* on your desk.

NOT:   Bella *had laid* her head on the desk.

YES:   Bella *had lain* her head on the desk.

### ■ EXERCISE FOR PRACTICE

In the sentences below, circle the correct form of the irregular verb. Check your answers at the end of this section.

Examples:   Bart has (bringed, (brought)) the boysenberries.

Bingo (has ate, (has eaten)) in the Student Union once too often.

((Lie,) lay) down and tell me your problem.

1. The bell has (rang, rung).
2. The auditors (have hidden, hided) the bankruptcy from the creditors.
3. Before we stopped for lunch, we (wrote, had wrote) the proposal.
4. Queenie has (blew, blown) her chance to be the Asparagus Princess.
5. Next year I will (sit, set) my goals higher.
6. Last night Hermione (seen, saw) her old boss at the bistro.
7. They had (began, begun) the meeting when I arrived.
8. The shirt is (wove, woven) of camel hair.
9. Biff has (stole, stolen) Buffy's heart.
10. The IRS (speaked, spoke) well of you in their report.
11. Please (lay, lie) the couch down before you (lie, lay) on it.
12. Cookie has (wore, worn) out her welcome.
13. Steven's shirt (shrank, shrunk) seven sizes.
14. Next month I (go, will go) to Peoria.
15. By the time Bilbo arrived, we (heard, had heard) the news.

## Adjective Avenue

> *Modifiers, even those clad only in their Calvin Klein jeans, should snuggle up to the word or phrase they modify.*
>
> William Safire

An **adjective** is a word that describes a noun, and occasionally, a pronoun. It usually answers one of the following questions: *What kind, how many, which one,* or *whose*? Adjectives are often called **modifiers.**

|  | Adjective | Adjective and Noun |
|---|---|---|
| **What kind?** | positive | positive attitude |
|  | green | green soup |
|  | spooky | spooky Halloween |
|  | fierce | fierce competition |
|  | left | left turn |
| **How many?** | some | some sense |
|  | all | all employees |
|  | six | six professors |
|  | many | many contracts |
| **Which one?** | this | this vampire |
|  | these | these peaches |
|  | that | that armadillo |
|  | those | those rejects |
| **Whose?** | its | its nest |
|  | their | their futures |
|  | manager's | manager's responsibility |
|  | my | my friend |
|  | anybody's | anybody's guess |

*Adjective test:* A word is an adjective if it makes sense with the word *thing* or *things*.

Your things; sweet young thing; wild thing; this old thing

### Putting an Adjective in Its Place

In the English language adjectives usually appear in front of the nouns or pronouns that they are describing. They either describe or limit the noun. **Descriptive adjectives** give color and brightness to the persons, places, or things they are describing. **Limiting adjectives** indicate how many, how much, which one, or whose.

The *large* crate contained a *packing* slip, a *current* invoice and *three* flashlamps.

*Large, packing,* and *current* are **descriptive adjectives**. *Three* is a **limiting adjective**.

## ■ EXERCISE FOR PRACTICE

In the following sentences, underline the adjective and decide whether it is descriptive or limiting. Put a **D** on the line for descriptive and an **L** on the line for limiting. Check your answers at the end of this section.

Examples:  __D__   Do not run the <u>power</u> supply over the limit.

__L__   The meeting will be held in <u>two</u> weeks.

1. _____ The waist is a terrible thing to mind. *Ziggy*

2. _____ Two branches of the company are moving to Zaire.

3. _____ Never hire an electrician with scorched eyebrows.

4. _____ A negotiation is a shared task.

5. _____ I would like three pickles on my sandwich.

## When Nouns Are Adjectives

Nouns are often used as adjectives, as in the following sentence:

A *telephone* headset allows you to move freely.

In this example *telephone* is an adjective because it tells you what kind of headset. Parts of speech are determined by how and where words are used in sentences. Even though *telephone* is usually a **common noun,** it is used as an adjective in this sentence. In the following sentence, notice that **proper nouns** are also used as adjectives.

The new *American* dream is a *German* automobile, a *Japanese* stereo, and a bottle of *French* champagne.

## ■ EXERCISE FOR PRACTICE

In the following exercise, underline the common and proper nouns used as adjectives. The number in parentheses tells how many nouns are used as adjectives in each sentence. Check your answers at the end of this section.

Examples:   Andrew's rule was to read the Sunday paper first. (2)

Jean-Louis' desk lamp is a museum piece. (3)

1. The government office is open until 9:00 on Friday night. (2)
2. Nigel's vacation is scheduled after the summer holidays. (2)
3. The mail clerk delivered the morning mail to the executive offices. (3)
4. Never let your classroom studies interfere with your college education. (2)
5. Holiday treats were candy canes and plum puddings. (3)

## PREDICATE ADJECTIVES

Sometimes adjectives lurk in predicates (the verb part of the sentence) following linking verbs. Adjectives that complete the meaning of the verb and modify the subject are called **predicate adjectives**. Predicate adjectives usually describe the subject noun.

> Computer programmers are *lovable*.

> The mechanics have become very *careless*.

## ■ EXERCISE FOR PRACTICE

Underline the predicate adjectives in the following sentences. On the line at the right, indicate the noun that the predicate adjective modifies. Check your answers at the end of this section.

Examples:   The false alarms were annoying.  alarms

Jean Luke seems restless. Jean Luke

The chemical spill in the lab proved harmless.  spill

1. During the earthquake, Corazon remained calm. _____
2. The new carpeting in the employees' lounge is attractive. _____
3. The October weather has been mild until now. _____

4. The secretaries are always rushed. _____

5. Fish that swim with the stream are dead. _____

---

**HELPFUL HINT:** If you aren't sure that a word is an adjective, look at the ending. Many adjectives come from nouns and other parts of speech. The following chart helps you to identify endings that change other parts of speech into adjectives.

---

| Nouns, Etc. | Endings | Adjectives |
|---|---|---|
| work (noun or verb) | -able | workable |
| region | -al | regional |
| wool | -en | woolen |
| use | -ful | useful |
| photograph | -ic | photographic |
| child | -ish | childish |
| restrict (verb) | -ive | restrictive |
| hope | -less | hopeless |
| danger | -ous | dangerous |
| fun | -y | funny |

## OTHER ADJECTIVES

**Interrogative adjectives** ask questions.

*Whose* committee made that decision?

*What* appliance does not work better when you plug it in?

*Why* is it taking so long for you to bring out my best qualities?

*Where* is the key to the executive washroom?

**Articles** are adjectives. Technically, *a, an,* and *the* are adjectives, but they are called articles. Articles can always be used with nouns, but beware of words that come between articles and their nouns.

*The* final <u>act</u> was mercifully short.

*A* very large <u>ego</u> stands in his way.

*The* is a **definite article**: "the desk" means one desk in particular.

We watched *the* Blue Angels from *the* Presidio.

*The* can refer to both singular and plural nouns.

*The* squid swam the back stroke.

(*Squid* is singular or plural here.)

*The* receptionist asks for identification.

*The* receptionists ask for identification.

*A* and *and* are **indefinite articles**. Use them when you don't need to specify anything or anyone in particular. "*A* squid" can be any squid. "*An* ego" can be any ego. Use *a* before nouns that begin with consonants: *a* chili pepper; *a* sardine. Use *an* before words that begin with vowel sounds.

| | |
|---|---|
| *an* agreement | *an* atrium |
| *an* employee | *an* eagle |
| *an* idea | *an* insert |
| *an* order | *an* oaf |

*an* hour (The *h* is silent, so you hear the vowel sound *o*.)

*an* update (Words beginning with *u* can be tricky; if the *u* is short, as in *update* or *undertow*, use *an*; if the *u* is long, as in *unit* or *Ukrainian*, use *a*.)

### ■ EXERCISE FOR PRACTICE

Write *a* or *an* in the blanks in the following sentences. Check your answers at the end of this section.

Examples:   Maxim would like __a__ unicorn for a pet.

As a new manager, Sarah was in __an__ awkward position.

1. ____ representative from personnel provided ____ new manual on how to be spontaneous.

2. Zeitel is catching ____ airplane this afternoon.

3. Our team won ____ trip to ____ island as ____ prize.

4. We also won ____ undisclosed amount of cash.

5. ''____ eye for ____ eye'' could be unsightly.

6. Yves has ____ uncle, ____ aunt, and ____ cousin working in his department.

# Using Adjectives Effectively

> *As for books that say to keep sentences short, cut out all adjectives, don't use dashes—I simply ignore them.*
>
> Alistaire Cooke

### Adjectives Are a Matter of Degree

A short adjective (one or sometimes two syllables) may change form to show the degree or extent to which the noun it modifies possesses the quality described by the adjective.

| Positive | Comparative | Superlative |
|---|---|---|
| (the simplest form) | (comparing two things or persons) | (comparing three or more things or persons) |
| heavy | heavier | heaviest |
| fine | finer | finest |
| small | smaller | smallest |
| silly | sillier | silliest |

Longer adjectives use *more* or *most* in front of the adjective to show comparison.

| Positive | Comparative | Superlative |
|---|---|---|
| famous | more famous | most famous |
| difficult | more difficult | most difficult |
| handsome | more handsome | most handsome |
| delicate | more delicate | most delicate |

Don't use *more* with short comparative forms of adjectives, and don't use *most* with short superlative forms.

NOT: Your calculator is *more better* than mine.

YES: Your calculator is *better* than mine.

NOT: Adrienne wears the *most bizarrest* clothes I have ever seen.

YES: Adrienne wears the *most bizarre* clothes I have ever seen.

## IRREGULAR ADJECTIVES

Some adjectives are called **irregular adjectives** because they change form considerably from one degree to the next: *many, more, most*. Rhyme or reason is out the window here, so you will have to study these changes carefully in order to recognize them easily. If you are uncertain about the degree of any adjective, check your dictionary.

| Positive | Comparative | Superlative |
|----------|-------------|-------------|
| bad | worse | worst |
| far | further | furthest |
| good, well | better | best |
| little | less | least |
| many, much | more | most |
| out | outer | outermost (or *far out*, if you're hip) |

## INCOMPARABLE ADJECTIVES

Some adjectives cannot be compared because the positive form expresses the only degree possible. For instance, if a circle is absolutely round, it can't be *more* round; if a gasoline tank is empty, it can't be *more* empty. Following are some adjectives that are not usually compared.

| | | | |
|---|---|---|---|
| perfect | unique | fatal | universal |
| alone | dead | wrong | straight |
| blind | final | vertical | right |

Degrees of adjectives can be confusing because the rules are unruly. Use your ear and listen for what sounds right. Adjectives such as *crisp* may be forever in the ''twilight zone'' of rules for proper English. Is it *crisp, crisper, crispest*, or is it *crisp, more crisp, most crisp*? (If you find the answer, please inform our publisher.)

## ■ EXERCISE FOR PRACTICE

Fill in the blanks with the correct comparative and superlative degrees of adjectives. Check your answers at the end of this section.

| | Positive | Comparative | Superlative |
|---|---|---|---|
| 1. | calm | | |
| 2. | cautious | | |
| 3. | final | | |
| 4. | good | | |
| 5. | valuable | | |
| 6. | wrong | | |
| 7. | able | | |
| 8. | far | | |
| 9. | easy | | |
| 10. | noisy | | |
| 11. | complete | | |
| 12. | famous | | |

## ■ EXERCISE FOR PRACTICE

In the following paragraph, circle each adjective and article. The number of adjectives in each sentence is indicated. Check your answers at the end of this section.

Example: To become (a) (competent) employee, learn (the) (gentle) art of (telephone) communication. You will save (many) hours of (valuable) time by learning (a) (few) (simple) (telephone) (contact) skills. (12)

When answering the office telephone, project a positive image with a pleasant voice. (6) Speak clearly, with a friendly smile on your face. (3) Set a specific personal goal to improve your company's image as a result of each conversation. (7) Learn to ask intelligent questions, then listen to your caller's answers. (3) Try not to transfer calls if you can give a responsible answer yourself. (2) When you must ask callers to hold, use their names, and give them a specific choice. (3)

"Mr. Swinn, would you care to wait, or would you like for me to call you back with that information?" (1) Remember that you *are* the company to outside callers. (2) They will judge your company as good or bad, and they may make important buying decisions based solely on your pleasant voice and good manners—or lack of them. (8)

## Adverb Alley

> *Get it done!*
> *Do it now!*
> *Adverbs tell when,*
> *What extent, where, and how.*

Like their cousin the adjective, **adverbs** are also modifiers. Adverbs usually end in *ly* (mostly, usually, really, happily, strongly), but some do not (not, just, too, very). Adverbs modify verbs, adjectives, and other adverbs.

| | |
|---|---|
| <u>Adverbs modifying verbs:</u> | Dr. Zang *always* provides examples in his lectures. |
| | Marmaduke behaved *badly* in the pet show. |
| <u>Adverbs modifying adjectives:</u> | There are *very* few people who don't become *more* interesting when they stop talking. |
| | The merger proved *too* difficult. |
| <u>Adverbs modifying other adverbs:</u> | You arrived *so* quickly. |
| | Dear Lord, give me patience, *right* now! |

Adverbs answer such questions as *where, when, how,* or *to what extent*. To test an adverb, ask yourself what word it is modifying and what question it is answering. Some examples of sentences with adverbs follow:

I never go *anywhere* without my shadow. (Where?)

Juan Antonio spoke *mysteriously*. (How?)

We *barely* made our deadline. (To what extent?)

Caleb needs the copies *now*. (When?)

Here is a list of adverbs that answer the questions *how, when, where,* or *to what extent.* Some end in *ly* and others do not.

| Where | When | To What Extent |
|---|---|---|
| where | often | almost |
| nowhere | soon | hardly |
| anywhere | now | too |
| somewhere | then | very |
| here | still | quite |
| there | when | really |
| down | never | all |
| backward | yet | as |
| forward | eventually | but (only) |
| around | already | equally |
| above | | even |

**How**

well

thus

justly

so

outrageously

quickly

anyway

## ■ EXERCISE FOR PRACTICE

In the following exercise, underline the adverbs in each sentence. The number at the end of the sentence tells you how many adverbs each sentence contains. Check your answers at the end of this section.

Examples:   The job took <u>only</u> two hours. (1)

The seaside town was <u>so</u> boring that when the tide went <u>out</u> it <u>never</u> came <u>back</u>. (4)

1. Completing the project within two weeks was much too difficult. (2)

2. This fine suit suits me just fine. (2)

3. Inform the committee that communications have totally broken down. (1)

4. Management sincerely encourages the quality movement. (1)

5. Everyone at the meeting, consciously or unconsciously, realized the importance of an accurate sales forecast. (2)

6. Christopher seemed to get good grades almost effortlessly. (2)

7. Our questionnaire takes only moments to complete. (1)

8. I only hope that the goals I never achieved were not really worth achieving. (4)

**NOTE:** In the sentences above, notice that you could eliminate most of the adverbs without changing the meaning of the sentences. Mark Twain put it delicately when he said, ''Kill the adverbs and the adjectives!'' Use these modifiers SPARINGLY in business writing. They weaken, rather than strengthen, your written communication.

## Using Adverbs Effectively

> *Perfect English is the slang of snobs.*
> With apologies to George Eliot

Some people are confused by the difference between adverbs and adjectives. The difference depends not so much on the ending of the word, but on the way the word is used in a sentence. If the word modifies a noun or a pronoun, it is an **adjective**. If it modifies a verb, an adjective or an adverb, it is an **adverb**.

Is Jessica *well*? (adjective)

Does Jessica play the piccolo *well*? (adverb)

Francoise made a *quick* turn. (adjective)

Francoise turned *quickly*. (adverb)

Many adverbs have a noun and an adjective form. The following list compares the three forms.

| Noun | Adjective | Adverb |
|------|-----------|--------|
| truth | truthful | truthfully |
| thanks | thankful | thankfully |
| hour | hourly | hourly |
| interest | interesting | interestingly |
| hope | hopeful | hopefully |

Some words keep the same form whether they are used as adjectives or adverbs.

| | | |
|------|------|-------|
| well | deep | right |
| early | fast | wrong |
| little | late | better |
| very | above | hard |
| much | long | |

## COMPARISON OF ADVERBS

Adverbs are compared, as adjectives are, to show different degrees of limiting or qualifying. Not as many adverbs as adjectives are capable of comparison. Most adverbs are compared by *more* or *most, less* or *least*. Some are compared by adding *er* or *est* to the end of the word.

| Positive | Comparative | Superlative |
|----------|-------------|-------------|
| easily | more easily | most easily |
| | less easily | least easily |
| quickly | more quickly | most quickly |
| | less quickly | least quickly |
| early | earlier | earliest |
| fast | faster | fastest |
| long | longer | longest |

Like some adjectives, some adverbs are irregular as well.

| Positive | Comparative | Superlative |
|----------|-------------|-------------|
| badly (ill) | worse | worst |
| far | farther | farthest |
| late | later | latest or last |
| much | more | most |
| close | closer | closest |
| well | better | best |
| little | less | least |

## ■ EXERCISE FOR PRACTICE

Underline the comparative and superlative degrees of the adverbs in the sentences below. Check your answers at the end of this section.

Examples:   The movie started <u>later</u> than we expected.

Compudek was the <u>least</u> likely company to feel the recession.

1. Penelope moves more quickly when her boss is around.
2. Alexis visits the home office less often than he used to.
3. Your customer service representative responded to our request most adequately.
4. Asking dumb questions is easier than correcting dumb mistakes.
5. I think I'll sit here and wait until my life gets better.
6. The pizza arrived earlier than we had planned.

# Preposition Place

> *It's your language too, buddy; if you want to abuse it and muddle it up, you will do that for yourself, not for me.*
>
> William Safire

*Pre* means *before*, so **preposition** means *before* position. Therefore, a preposition is a word in the position in front of a noun. Like a trusty guide, prepositions go before, or lead in, nouns and pronouns.

| | |
|---|---|
| *on* the seesaw | *to* the director |
| *in* the soup | *around* the mulberry bush |
| *from* an admirer | *of* the officers |

Here is a list of the most frequently used **simple prepositions**:

| | | |
|---|---|---|
| about | by | onto |
| above | concerning | out |
| across | despite | out of |
| after | down | outside |
| against | due to | since |
| along | during | through |
| among | for | throughout |
| at | from | to |
| before | into | toward |
| below | like | underneath |
| beneath | near(by) | until |
| beside(s) | of | up |
| between | off | with |
| beyond | on | without |

A simple test for prepositions is : ''I am talking _____ the trees. Try placing different prepositions in the blank space to see if they make sense. This works fairly well, unless you are not accustomed to talking to trees.

To spot a preposition, always look for the noun or pronoun that follows it. This noun or pronoun is called the **object of the preposition**. It answers the questions *what*? or *whom*?

Give the paperwork to the *foreman*.

*Foreman* is the noun following the preposition *to*. Therefore, *foreman* is the object of the preposition. It answers the question *To whom?*

## ■ EXERCISE FOR PRACTICE

Underline the object of the preposition in the following sentences. Refer to your list of prepositions if you aren't sure which words are prepositions. Check your answers at the end of this section.

Examples:  The receptionist won't be here on <u>Wednesday.</u>

When will Cuthbert be in the regional <u>office?</u>

The lake comes right to the <u>shore.</u>

1. Xi Chan wrote a letter about the late shipment.

2. Meet me after class.

3. Can you work until 6:00?

4. Computers were invented by Murphy.

5. Our boss is pleased with our progress.

6. To a pessimist, all surprises are pleasant.

A prepositional phrase may have more than two words in it. The noun or pronoun that is the object of the preposition may have one or more adjectives as modifiers.

Nori recorded the minutes *with a small tape recorder*.

The two adjectives *small* and *tape* modify the object of the preposition, *recorder*.

**Note to Nonnative Speakers:** You may find prepositions difficult because they did not occur in your primary language. There are no "quick fixes" (easy answers) to help a new speaker or writer. Be patient, listen carefully, read and notice, and ask for help. Finally, don't be afraid to try! Use English as much as possible. Gradually you will improve. Be sure that your expectations are realistic, and give yourself credit for what you have already learned.

# Using Prepositions Effectively

> *Be careful of the word you take*
> *Lest your word a prison make.*

## PREPOSITIONAL PITFALLS

### "Traditional Pairings"

You can avoid some problems with prepositions by learning which prepositions go together in pairs. Perhaps you will want to memorize the following group of prepositions. Some nouns, verbs, and adjectives are followed by a pet preposition, and only that preposition is correct—because it has always been that way. For example, the preposition used after the adjective *common* is *to*, as in this sentence:

> Stage fright is *common to* inexperienced speakers.

Following is a list of nouns, verbs, and adjectives and the traditional prepositions that accompany them:

| | | |
|---|---|---|
| abstain from | concerned with | jealous of |
| acquit of | consist of | oblivious of |
| addicted to | desire for | prerequisite to |
| adept in | desirous of | prior to |
| adhere to | detract from | proficient in |
| agree to (a thing) | devoid of | profit by |

| | | |
|---|---|---|
| agree with (a person) | differ from (things) | prohibit from |
| angry at (a thing) | differ in | protect against |
| angry with (a person) | differ with (a person) | reason with |
| averse to | different from | regret for |
| capable of | disagree with | rely on |
| center on | envious of | repugnant to |
| characteristic of | expert in | sensitive to |
| common to | foreign to | separate from |
| compare to (for an example) | hint at | substitute for |
| compare with (to illustrate a point) | identify with | superior to |
| | independent of | susceptible to |
| compatible with | infer from | sympathize with |
| concern in | inferior to | tamper with |
| concerned with | inseparable from | |

## ■ EXERCISE FOR PRACTICE

Study the list above until you are familiar with it, then test yourself by filling in the blanks in the following sentences with the correct preposition—without referring to the list. When you are finished, check your answers by referring to the list, or by checking the answers at the end of this section.

Examples:   Margot couldn't agree __to__ Yelma's terms.

All of the employees disagree __with__ the project goals.

Do you have a concern __in__ this matter?

1. I agree _____ the person who said that common sense is the least common of all the senses.

2. The problems center _____ the length of employees' lunch hours.

3. I am envious _____ Sophia Loren, who got where she is by eating spaghetti.

4. A student's desire _____ the fountain of knowledge brings him to college to drink.

5. Prior _____ the meeting, everyone had a different opinion.

6. My conclusion is different _____ yours.

7. I infer _____ your definite response that you mean "maybe."

8. Are you angry _____ Sarafina about your transfer?

## Unnecessary Prepositions

Sometimes extra prepositions are used in speaking and writing. Edit your speech and writing ruthlessly to avoid these grammar boo-boos.

NOT:   Jorge started in to file his taxes.

YES:   Jorge started to file his taxes.

OR

Jorge began to file his taxes.

NOT:   Take your hamster off of the hors d'oeuvres tray.

YES:   Take your hamster off the hors d'oeuvres tray.

NOT:   Where are you at?

YES:   Where are you?

## ■ EXERCISE FOR PRACTICE

Cross out the unnecessary prepositions in the following sentences. Check your answers at the end of this section.

Examples:   Never run alongside of a moving train.

We went like three blocks the wrong way.

Do you want to go with?

1. We finished up the meeting on time.

2. Let's sit down here.

3. Do you want to walk over to the cafeteria?

4. At about what time does "Star Trek" begin on TV?

5. Duffus tracked down the problem to the computer.

6. We found the spare parts inside of the drawer.

### Ending Sentences with Prepositions

A preposition may correctly be used as the last word in a sentence. Although a few purists may disagree, you can end a sentence with anything you choose (almost), including prepositions. English is not as formal as it was at one time, and in some cases you have little choice but to use a preposition to end a sentence.

> I was told to stand *by*.
>
> Whom did you send it *to*?
>
> Look *up*!
>
> Let's get it *on*.

Of course you do not want to abuse this flagrantly, so use common sense and avoid prepositional endings when you can do so easily. You can usually avoid the problem by rewriting the sentence.

> NOT:    Isaiah was the one by whom I was stood up for.
>
> YES:    Isaiah was the one who stood up for me.
>
> NOT:    A preposition is a word you shouldn't end a sentence with.
>
> YES:    You shouldn't end a sentence with a preposition.

### ■ EXERCISE FOR PRACTICE

Rewrite the following sentences so that they no longer end with prepositions. Check your answers at the end of this section.

Examples:   What did you do that for?
            Why did you do that?

            Where are you from?
            Where do you live?

1. Why was Bob the one you turned to?

_____

2. I resented my manager for leading me on.

_____

3. At the conference we had many issues to talk about.

_____

4. What are you hinting at?

_____

5. Morey is difficult to reason with.

_____

6. Sheila is someone I am envious of.

_____

# Conjunction Junction

*Don't give me any ifs, ands, or buts!*

The underlined words in the paragraph below are conjunctions. **Conjunctions** are connectors that join words, phrases, and clauses. In this section you will bump into four kinds of conjunctions: **coordinating conjunctions**, **correlative (paired) conjunctions**, **conjunctive adverbs**, and **subordinating conjunctions**.

> Not only Markie Margolis, but also Mack and Maggie were either for tassels or feathered boas on their perky new uniforms and sequined hats. Although they waited breathlessly, the decision was delayed and they returned to work, where they moped in silence.

## COORDINATING CONJUNCTIONS

The conjunctions you see most often are the **coordinating conjunctions** *but, or, yet, so, for, and,* and *nor*. You can remember them with this mnemonic: BOYS FAN

**But Or Yet So  For And Nor**

Here are examples of coordinating conjunctions used to join words, phrases and clauses.

Words:    Socorro ordered extra parts *and* supplies.

Phrases:    Send the charts to Mr. Beezer *or* to Mrs. Klemper.

Clauses:    I want to be respected, *but* I don't want to be respectable.

*On guard!* Conjunctions can be tricky! From previous exercises you may remember that a word can be more than one part of speech. Conjunctions are no exception. Only when the words *but, or, yet, so, for, and,* and *nor* join other words, phrases, or clauses are they considered conjunctions. *And, or,* and *nor* are the only words that are always conjunctions.

Preposition:     I understand all *but* ninety percent of the problem.

Conjunction:     The other person's idea is opinion, *but* your idea is truth.

Adverb:     I am waiting for the cows to come home; they haven't arrived *yet*.

Conjunction:     I expected the cows earlier; *yet* they haven't arrived.

### ■ EXERCISE FOR PRACTICE

Underline the coordinating conjunctions in each sentence below. Check your answers at the end of this section.

Examples:    Please visit me while I am fat <u>and</u> happy.

If you can't win, you should change the rules <u>or</u> abandon the game.

I helped my coworkers, <u>but</u> they weren't satisfied.

1. It isn't who you "know," but who you "yes."
2. Grover doesn't enjoy Cleveland, nor does George wish to visit Washington.
3. The managers and administrative assistants will meet next Wednesday.
4. Kari's desires were that she be nominated for a student office or that she be voted Homecoming Queen.
5. I recognize my body's need to get off the couch, yet I refuse to move.
6. Tyrone would have stayed afloat in management, but he made waves.

### CORRELATIVE CONJUNCTIONS

**Correlative conjunctions** are *pairs* of connecting words that also link words, phrases, and clauses. Here is a list of correlative conjunctions:

| | | |
|---|---|---|
| both – and | not only – but also | either – or |
| if – then | neither – nor | although – yet |
| whether – or | as – as | so – that |

Since these words are in pairs, the words they connect in sentences must be equal (parallel). Here's how they work.

*Either* I am mistaken *or* you are yawning.

*Neither* a borrower *nor* a lender be.

We are *not only* happy to have your business, *but also* glad to have a new friend.

*If* you can see that I am deceiving you, *then* I can't be deceiving you very effectively.

A general rule of punctuation for correlative conjunctions is that if the sentence is short and clear you do not need commas. For longer sentences, or for clarity, use a comma.

### ■ EXERCISE FOR PRACTICE

In the following sentences, underline the pairs of correlative conjunctions. Check your answers at the end of this section.

Examples:   Please decide <u>whether</u> you want to travel by plane <u>or</u> by train.

Farrah's temper was <u>not only</u> fiery, <u>but also</u> immediate.

1. My job was both to design the course and to teach it.

2. The committee will either avoid a decision or delay it.

3. If I didn't understand you, then I wouldn't disagree.

4. Both Rodney and Cara submitted their resignations.

5. Whether you or I are chosen to clean the windows in the envelopes is undecided.

6. Dominique wants to be as rich as the Queen of England.

7. The project was neither on schedule nor within budget.

8. If you didn't have problems, then you wouldn't need people around to solve them; however, if you didn't have people around, then you might not have the problems.

## CONJUNCTIVE ADVERBS

**Conjunctive adverbs** are like coordinating conjunctions in that they are also connectors. However, they are used to show the logical connection between two *independent clauses*.

> Spike showed great potential; *and for this reason,* he received the assignment.

Sometimes conjunctive adverbs introduce the second of two closely related independent clauses as a new sentence, as in this example:

> The auditor's report clarified the shortage. *Moreover,* the report was well written.

When independent clauses are joined to form a compound sentence, a semicolon is placed before, and a comma after, the conjunctive adverb. Some short sentences are clear without the comma.

> Our salespeople give their talents to the company; *however,* they give their genius to their expense accounts.

> We need to make some changes; *therefore* you change first.

Here is a list of conjunctive adverbs.

| | | |
|---|---|---|
| accordingly | however | on the contrary |
| as a result | in addition | on the other hand |
| consequently | in the first place | otherwise |
| for example | indeed | still |
| for this reason | likewise | therefore |
| furthermore | moreover | thus |
| hence | nevertheless | yet |

## ■ EXERCISE FOR PRACTICE

Join the following sets of independent clauses (simple sentences) with conjunctive adverbs to form one sentence. Use semicolons and commas as necessary. Check for possible answers at the end of this section.

Examples:  The program calls for additional resources; *as a result,*

*i*
̷At will be difficult to initiate.

Professor Rodriguez helped anyone who needed it; *for this reason,*

*h*
̷He was a popular instructor.

This world is such a tidy place; *on the other hand,*

*t*
̷There is always room for the untidy.

1. Beatrice works twelve hours a day. _____ She volunteers at the community center on Saturdays.

2. The factory representative complained about the shield assembly. _____ The foreman changed the procedure.

3. Vicente believes that education and hard work are the keys to success. _____ He attends night school and works two jobs.

4. Gaminio was a reluctant soldier. _____ He couldn't remember which side he was on.

5. The administration has designated certain nonsmoking areas. _____ You can smoke in your office and in the smoking lounges.

6. Dulcina wastes a lot of time. _____ She is creative about it.

## SUBORDINATING CONJUNCTIONS

Some sentences are composed of unequal parts. The main idea of a sentence is expressed in the *independent clause* (also called a **main clause**). Additional ideas that support, or give more information about, the independent clause are called *dependent clauses*. **Subordinating conjunctions** are words that introduce dependent clauses. Together an independent clause and a dependent clause form a **complex sentence**.

*If you like our service,* please refer us to others.

In this sentence, *If* is a **subordinating conjunction** that introduces the dependent clause, *"If you like our service"*; *"please refer us to others"* is the independent clause. In this example, the dependent clause comes before the independent clause, but in some sentences the dependent clause comes after the independent clause.

Subordinating conjunctions clarify time, compare ideas, tell how and where events occur, and explain cause-and-effect. Their jobs are to connect parts of sentences that are unequal. Following is a list of subordinating conjunctions.

| | | | |
|---|---|---|---|
| after | even though | that | wherever |
| although | except | then | whether |
| as | if | though | which |
| because | since | unless | who |
| before | so that | when | whom |
| even | than | where | whose |

In the following sentence the subordinating conjunction *before* introduces the dependent clause. Notice that the dependent clause follows the independent clause.

Let's go, *before they ask us to do something.*

Dependent clauses precede, follow, or squeeze between the subject and verb in independent clauses, as in this sentence:

The proposal, *which was rejected earlier,* was resubmitted.

### ■ EXERCISE FOR PRACTICE

In the following sentences circle the subordinating conjunction and underline the dependent clause that it introduces in each sentence. Check your answers at the end of this section.

Examples: (When) you eat Italian food, you are hungry again in five or six days.

(If) you have to tell people (that) you are famous, you're not famous.

Please find storage space (before) the shipment arrives.

1. As you may know, I have experience in sales, marketing, and distribution.

2. Minoru fixed the bookkeeping problem so that it would not recur.

3. Although I have enjoyed my job, I have decided to go back to college.

4. The team that completes the project with zero defects will receive a large bonus.

5. The lab reported progress, until the contents of the test tubes took on a life of their own.

6. Because Omar's son was graduating, he requested personal leave time.

## ■ REVIEW EXERCISES FOR PRACTICE (PARTS OF SPEECH)

Identify the following groups of words as **nouns, pronouns, verbs, adjectives, adverbs, prepositions,** or **conjunctions.** Check your answers at the end of this section.

1. _____ however, yet, because, that, either-or, then, on the other hand

2. _____ blockhead, microscope, Dallas, navy, scourge, heat, vision, Francisco

3. _____ wildly, very, not, wantonly, just, often, suddenly, around, carefully

4. _____ run, had been bounced, are, bite, shall, whittle, will have been forgiven

5. _____ himself, someone, me, whose, them, you, hers, whom, nobody, something

6. _____ sincere, spoiled, some, single, those, bald, rich, everybody's, an, smallest

## ■ REVIEW EXERCISE

In the following sentence, find as many of the parts of speech as you can and list them below. Check your answers at the end of this section.

Engineers catch misspellings only in documents written by someone who is not an engineer; accordingly, any errors will be discovered only after the final copy of the document is carefully bound and mailed.

Nouns: _____

Pronouns: _____

Verbs: _____

Adjectives (including articles): _____

Adverbs: _____

Prepositional Phrases: _____

Conjunctions: _____

## ■ REVIEW EXERCISE

Identify the parts of speech—nouns, pronouns, verbs, adverbs, adjectives, prepositions, conjunctions—of the underlined words in each of the following sentences. Check your answers at the end of this section.

Examples:    __pronouns__    Edgar and I discussed our prospects.

     __nouns__    Pet rocks and hoola hoops were passing fancies.

   __conjunctions__    Neither Effie nor Delfino would challenge Bart and Sue.

1. _____ On Wednesday the doctor removed a piece of cartilage about the size of New Hampshire from my knee.

2. _____ Aron raced to the mailbox, dropped his tax returns into the slot, and breathed a sigh of relief.

3. _____ We appreciate your letter and we are glad that you like our products and our service.

4. _____ Not only Yashuhiro, but also Yoshiyuki will join Trudee and me when we go to Indonesia.

5. _____ With whom are you going to the movie?

6. _____ With whom are you going to the movie?

7. _____ Never let a mechanical object know that you are in a hurry.

8. _____ Spiro did not work effectively to change the very inefficient system.

9. _____ Neither Ruben nor Frank could find a manager, but they found a supervisor before the problem became serious.

10. _____ Sitting at his desk with his feet up, Holden felt strongly motivated by a lack of desire.

# Answers for Section I

## NOUNS

Page 3

The following words should be circled: trucker, astronaut, owl, nerd, college, locker, workbench, cabbage, coward, dragon.

Page 3

1. Australia

2. Despina, CNN

3. Human Resources Department, English, Spanish, Japanese

Page 4

1. common:  office, forms, engineers

   proper:  Otis, Peoria

2. common:  visitors, plant

   proper:  Monday, India, Taiwan, New Orleans

3. common:  dollars, research, development

   proper:  Acme Designs, January, June

4. common:  bats, kittens, creatures, kitchen

   proper  Katherine Krump, Staten Island

5. common:  executives

   proper:  Toyotas, Hondas

Page 8

1. brothers-in-law.  2. cactus, cactuses, or cacti.  3. lives.  4. oxen.  5. handfuls.
6. zeroes.  7. measles.  8. fungi or funguses.

Page 9

1. P, child.  2. S, fleeces.  3. S, Smiths.  4. S, ladies.  5. P, pea.  6. S, secretaries.
7. S, comedies.  8. P, ox.  9. P, coat.  10. S, geese.  11. S, mothers-in-law.
12. S, thousands.  13. S, boxes.  14. P, scarf.

Page 10

1. goddess' or goddess's.  2. moose's.  3. copier's.  4. employee's.  5. dress' or dress's.  6. Mr. Jones' or Mr. Jones's.  7. hero's.  8. story's.  9. pension's. 10. Bess' or Bess's.

Page 11

1. churches'.  2. customers'.  3. sheep's.  4. savings's or savings'.  5. classes'. 6. warranties'.  7. unions'.  8. feet's.  9. reports'.  10. Joneses'.

## PRONOUNS

Page 13

1. their        2. its        3. her        4. its        5. their
6. it

Page 14

1. I, that, you, nothing

2. you, me, your

3. I, that, I, I, I, him

4. Some, my, me, I, myself

5. this, my

6. I, anyone, me

7. Everyone, his, her

8. I('m), anybody else, who

9. Our, everyone

10. We, our, our

Page 16

1. I.  2. he.  3. us.  4. its.  5. he, his.  6. its.  7. who.  8. him.
9. me, who.  10. its.

## VERBS

Page 19

1. unloaded (truck)

2. supports (program)

3. changed (lock)

4. left (shoes)

5. Forgive (me )

Page 20

1. cheered. 2. was. 3. Sit. 4. went. 5. gossiped. 6. is, is. 7. improved.
8. are. 9. have been working. 10. will be.

Page 21

1. P, I. 2. A, I. 3. A, T. 4. A, I. 5. P, I. 6. P, I. 7. A, I. 8. A, I.
9. A, T. 10. P, I.

Page 23

1. was. 2. is. 3. has been. 4. were. 5. taste. 6. will be. 7. seem.
8. feels. 9. are. 10. is.

Page 25

1. should receive. 2. will show. 3. has given. 4. would have confused.
5. will be routing. 6. have told. 7. will be completing. 8. is serving.
9. has been behaving. 10. has issued.

Page 29

1. <u>way</u> (is)

2. <u>Angel</u> (wants)

3. <u>truth</u> (comes)

4. <u>People</u> (are)

5. <u>hero</u> (steps)

6. <u>time</u> (is)

Page 31

1. used. 2. refuses. 3. will recommend. 4. recovered. 5. will tend.
6. requires. 7. will need. 8. contained. 9. hinders. 10. will need.

Page 33

1. had learned. 2. have inspired. 3. will have earned. 4. have designed.
5. will have rolled. 6. had acquired. 7. have guessed. 8. had forgotten.
9. have listened. 10. had cross-trained.

Page 40

1. rung. 2. have hidden. 3. wrote. 4. blown. 5. set. 6. saw. 7. begun.
8. woven. 9. stolen. 10. spoke. 11. lay, lie. 12. worn. 13. shrank.
14. will go. 15. had heard.

## ADJECTIVES

Page 42

1.  _D_ terrible.  2.  _L_ Two.  3.  _D_ Scorched.  4.  _D_ shared.  5.  _L_ three.

Page 43

1. government, Friday

2. Nigel's, summer

3. mail, morning, executive

4. classroom, college

5. Holiday, candy, plum

Page 43

1. calm, Corazon

2. attractive, carpeting

3. mild, weather

4. rushed, secretaries

5. dead, fish

Page 45

1. A, a.  2. an.  3. a, an, a.  4. an.  5. An, an.  6. an, an, a.

Page 48

| Positive | Comparative | Superlative |
| --- | --- | --- |
| 1. calm | calmer | calmest |
| 2. cautious | more cautious | most cautious |
| 3. final | final | final |
| 4. good | better | best |
| 5. valuable | more valuable | most valuable |
| 6. wrong | wrong | wrong |
| 7. able | abler | ablest |
| 8. far | further | furthest |

Page 48 (cont.)

| | | |
|---|---|---|
| 9. easy | easier | easiest |
| 10. noisy | noisier | noisiest |
| 11. complete | more complete | most complete |
| 12. famous | more famous | most famous |

Page 48

When answering (the) (office) telephone, project (a) (positive) image with (a) (pleasant) voice. (6) Speak clearly, with (a) (friendly) smile on (your) face. (3) Set (a) (specific) (personal) goal to improve (your) (company's) image as (a) result of (each) conversation. (7) Learn to ask (intelligent) questions, then listen to (your) (caller's) answers. (3) Try not to transfer calls if you can give (a) (responsible) answer yourself. (2) When you must ask callers to hold, use (their) names, and give them (a) (specific) choice. (3) "Mr. Swinn, would you care to wait, or would you like for me to call you back with (that) information?" (1) Remember that you *are* (the) company to (outside) callers. (2) They will judge (your) company as (good) or (bad,) and they may make (important) (buying) decisions based solely on (your) (pleasant) voice and (good) manners—or lack of them. (8)

## ADVERBS

Page 51

1. much too
2. just fine
3. totally
4. sincerely
5. consciously, unconsciously
6. almost effortlessly
7. only
8. only, never, not really

Page 53

1. more quickly.  2. less often.  3. most adequately.  4. easier.  5. better.
6. earlier.

## PREPOSITIONS

Page 55

1. shipment.  2. class.  3. 6:00.  4. Murphy.  5. progress.  6. pessimist.

Page 57

1. with.  2. on.  3. of.  4. for.  5. to.  6. from.  7. from.  8. with.

Page 58

Eliminate the following words: 1. up.  2. down.  3. over.  4. At about. 5. down.  6. of.

Page 59

Suggested rewrites:

1. Why did you turn to Bob?

2. I resented my manager for deceiving me.

3. At the conference we had many issues to discuss.

4. What are you suggesting?

5. I have difficulty reasoning with Morey.

6. I am envious of Sheila.

## CONJUNCTIONS

Page 61

1. but.  2. nor.  3. and.  4. or.  5. yet.  6. but.

Page 62

1. both–and      5. whether–or

2. either–or      6. as–as

3. If–then        7. neither–nor

4. Both–and      8. If–then; if–then (*however* is a conjunctive adverb)

Page 64

Possible ways to use conjunctive adverbs to join two sentences:

1. Beatrice works twelve hours a day; in addition, she volunteers at the community center on Saturdays.

2. The factory representative complained about the shield assembly; for this reason, the foreman changed the procedure.

3. Vicente believes that education and hard work are the keys to success; thus, he attends night school and works two jobs.

4. Gaminio was a reluctant soldier; furthermore, he couldn't remember which side he was on.

5. The administration has designated certain nonsmoking areas; for example, you can smoke in your office and in the smoking lounges.

6. Dulcina wastes a lot of time; however, she is creative about it.

Page 65

1. (As) you may know.
2. (so that) it would not recur.
3. (Although) I have enjoyed my job
4. (that) completes the project with zero defects
5. (until) the contents of the test tubes took on a life of their own.
6. (Because) Omar's son was graduating

**REVIEW EXERCISES**

Page 66

1. conjunctions.  2. nouns.  3. adverbs.  4. verbs.  5. pronouns.  6. adjectives.

Page 66

Nouns: engineers, misspellings, documents, engineer, errors, copy, document
Pronouns: someone, who
Verbs: catch, written, is, will be discovered, is bound, mailed

Page 66 (cont.)

Adjectives: an, any, the, final, the

Adverbs: only, not, carefully

Prepositional phrases: in documents, by someone, after the final copy, of the document

Conjunctions: accordingly, and

Page 67

1. prepositions.  2. verbs.  3. nouns.  4. conjunctions.  5. prepositions.
6. pronouns.  7. verbs.  8. adverbs.  9. conjunctions.  10. prepositions.

# Chapter II

# Sentence Sense

# Sentence Sense

*This is the best advice I know to improve your writing. Don't block the flow of the sentence.*

Andy Arbuckle.

If you can write a clear, correct sentence, you can write anything: business letters, job applications, term papers, hit songs, or short stories. To write a good sentence you must follow these two rules. If you do not, a dragon will eat you.

1. Every sentence must contain a subject and a verb (also called a predicate).

2. A sentence must express a complete thought.

In writing, a sentence begins with a capital letter and ends with a period, a question mark, or an exclamation point.

| Subject | Predicate |
|---------|-----------|
| Farina Farnaby | is queen of the Eggplant Festival. |
| Office politics | can be fierce! |
| In March, three employees | won awards for outstanding service. |

## RECOGNIZING SENTENCES

A complete sentence has at least one subject and one predicate. The **subject** is the person or thing that the sentence is talking about. The **predicate** is the verb and its modifiers. The predicate tells what the subject is or does. Modifiers are words that describe or support.

A **simple subject** is the naked noun or pronoun without modifiers.

The math *test* was difficult.

*Everyone* attended the company picnic.

Last Wednesday my *manager* found extra money in the budget.

**NOTE:** Some sentences begin with command verbs, so the subject is not apparent. In this case, the subject is understood to be *you*. *You* is an implied subject.

(You) Hold this hot potato.

(You) Write me a memo.

(You) Please pass the pretzels.

**Compound subjects** contain two or more simple subjects connected by *and, or,* or *nor*. They share the same verb.

*Nature* and *I* abhor a vacuum.

A *check* or *money order* must be enclosed with your application.

Neither *rain* nor *sleet* nor aching *feet* keep the postman from his beat.

The **complete subject** is the simple subject and its supporting modifiers.

*A former employee in the shipping department* built pigeon perches above the front door.

*The kind gentleman who signs my checks* added a small bonus this month.

*Several long black limousines* are blocking your Edsel.

The **predicate** always contains a verb. The **simple predicate** is the verb or verb phrase without any modifiers.

Dentists *should have* more patience.

Our secretary *found* an old typewriter in the storeroom.

I *have been waiting* for the shipment for two weeks.

The **complete predicate** is the verb and its supporting modifiers.

My friends *did not return from swimming at Crocodile Lake.*

Our manager, Mrs. Sweeny, *believes in meeting her deadlines, no matter how long it takes.*

After two weeks, we *abandoned the new software program.*

A **compound predicate** is two or more simple predicates connected by *and, or,* or *nor.* Both predicates belong to the same subject.

The shelf *tipped* and *fell* under the weight of the books.

*Did* you *see* the game, or *hear* who won?

I neither *drove* the car nor *dented* the fender.

---

Dear Grandma Marian,

When I write letters or memos I always use complete sentences. When I speak, however, I don't always express my ideas as complete thoughts. Should I strive for complete sentences when I speak?

Nada Klu

Dear Nada,

You do not always have to use complete sentences when you speak. Spoken English is more relaxed and informal than written English. When writing, you should follow grammar rules and write complete sentences. When you speak you use not only words, but also nonverbal communication (body language) and tone of voice (inflection) to convey your message. Statistics indicate that tone and body language tell us more than words do. However, this information should not be an excuse for sloppy speaking. Here is an example of a typical conversation you might hear between two people who need coaching in good speaking habits:

*Joe:* ''Whachadoin, Moe?'' (Eyebrow arched, voice trails up.)

*Moe:* ''Nutin. Whachoodoon?'' (Blink, tic, snort.)

*Joe:* ''Namuch. Wannagitsumpnteet?'' (Arches eyebrow, pats tummy.)

When you speak, use LOMM: Large, Open, Moving Mouth. Take a moment to think. Ask yourself what you want your listener to know. Mentally organize your information, make eye contact, and speak as you would like to be spoken to. Yes, complete sentences are helpful, but few people use them consistently.

Grandma

### ■ EXERCISE FOR PRACTICE

In the following sentences underline the simple subjects with one line and the simple predicates with two lines. Check your answers at the end of this section.

Examples: Huck Finn wandered along the Mississippi.

In two weeks Frick and Frack will be taking their history finals.

Mr. Mills bought a new desktop computer, then gave his old one to his son.

1. Ezra pounded his fists on the desk.
2. One partridge and two pear trees disappeared from the Christmas inventory.
3. Our new accountant has more dollars than sense.
4. Ziggy bought a new car last night and hit a police van this morning.
5. Aliens visited the school library and the administration office.

In the following sentences underline the complete subject with one line and the complete predicate with two lines. Check your answers at the end of this section.

Examples: The common names of plants and animals are not capitalized in writing.

The largest cities in California are Los Angeles and San Jose.

The sales support people in Des Moines are getting restless.

1. By the end of the week our tired team completed the demanding project.
2. Bimbo and Bimbette, the Branson twins, live in a make-believe world.
3. Wild horses couldn't make me bungee jump.
4. I studied for the quiz for six hours.
5. Managers who support their employees' professional growth are good mentors.

# Four Kinds of Sentences

> *Proof carefully in case you any words out.*
>
> —Jan Venolia

Sentences fulfill four functions. Most commonly they make statements (**declarative**). They also ask questions (**interrogative**); they give orders (**imperative**); and they express emotion (**exclamatory**). Here are examples of each kind of sentence.

| | |
|---|---|
| **Declarative** (a statement) | I made a mistake. |
| **Interrogative** (a question) | Do you make mistakes? |
| **Imperative** (a command or strong request) | Stop making mistakes. |
| **Exclamatory** (an expression of emotion) | I'm sorry! |

### ■ EXERCISE FOR PRACTICE

Identify the types of sentences below by using the following initials:

   **D** Declarative     **INT** Interrogative     **IMP** Imperative     **E** Exclamatory

Check your answers at the end of this section.

Examples:    _D_  Misha is not a happy camper.

   _INT_ What's wrong, Misha?

   _IMP_ Take me home.

   _E_  I hate bugs!

1. _____ You must pay the rent.

2. _____ Is that the new accountant who is counting beans at his desk?

3. _____ Let's discuss my problems.

4. _____ Forget it!

5. _____ To write simply is not simple.

6. _____ What shall I do until you change your bad habits?

7. _____ Come in and eat before we both starve! (*Sign in restaurant window*)

8. _____ No way!

# A Brief Pause for the Phrase and the Clause

> *Five o'clock tea served at all hours.*
> —Sign in the window of a Berlin cafe.

Sentences are easy to write when we understand how they are constructed. All sentences are combinations of phrases and clauses. A clause is a group of words that contains a subject and a predicate, and a phrase is a group of words that supports the subject or predicate in a clause. Let's look at phrases first.

## It Pays to Phrase

All of the underlined groups of words below are **phrases**. These groups of words go together because they express a single idea. They provide details that make sentences interesting. Phrases can contain a subject or a verb; however, they do not contain both.

> English is one of 1500 languages that is spoken by the 5 billion people on the planet Earth. Being a speaker of English does not guarantee that you will understand others who also speak your language. Accents, dialects and occupational jargon cause difficulty for those who wish to converse with one another even in the same language. Being Australian may prevent you from understanding a resident of Toledo, Ohio.

Phrases come in many colors and styles, including **prepositional phrases, verb phrases,** and **verbals (infinitive, gerund,** and **participial phrases)**. Following are examples of each.

**Prepositional phrase.** A prepositional phrase contains a preposition (see pages 56–57 for a list of prepositions) and an object. The object is a noun or a pronoun. Prepositional phrases are used as nouns, adjectives, and adverbs.

> Wombats are sleeping *in the spare bedroom*. (adverb)

> *On Wednesday* (adverb), two visitors *from Burma* (adjective) will visit our manufacturing plant *in Brussels* (adjective).

> *In the afternoon* is a good time to call. (noun)

**Verb phrases.** A verb phrase is an action word (a verb) and its helpers. Helping verbs express the tense of the verb (the time that an action takes place).

Delilah *has been thinking* of quitting her job.

You *should force* yourself to relax more often.

Mongo *will be using* the fax machine on Monday.

**Verbal phrases.** Verbal phrases are the children of verbs. There are three kinds: **infinitive, gerund,** and **participial.**

**Infinitive phrase** (*to* + verb + an object or a modifier, or both). An infinitive phrase can be used as a noun, an adjective, or an adverb.

My goal is *to save the world* (noun), while I continue *to lead a nice life.* (adverb).

*To pass my exams* is my goal. (noun)

I have an idea *to discuss with you.* (adjective)

**Gerund phrase** (*ing* form of verb + object or modifiers, or both). Gerund phrases are always used as nouns. In the first and third examples below they are used as the subjects of the sentences.

*Living well* is the best revenge.

My manager encourages *working as a team.*

*Your cooking* is quite interesting.

**Participial phrase.** (*ing* or *ed* form of verb + object + modifiers, or both). A participial phrase is always used as an adjective to modify a noun or a pronoun.

**NOTE:** Because a participial phrase is an adjective, it cannot be used as the subject of a sentence. In the following examples, the participial phrase tells you something about the subject, but it is not the subject itself.

The woman *filling out the forms* is our new vendor.

*Having read the minutes,* Wilhelm sat down.

*Outraged by Rambo's contempt,* Elvira shouted, ''I am in charge of my life! Is that okay with you?''

■ **EXERCISE FOR PRACTICE**

Identify the underlined phrase in each of the sentences below by using the following code:

VP  Verb phrase      PP  Prepositional phrase

Check your answers at the end of this section.

Examples:  PP   Technical reports describe the results <u>of scientific research</u>.

VP   You <u>should be tempted</u> by my offer.

PP   Most <u>of our customers</u> request this product.

VP   Juan Chavez <u>will graduate</u> at the end of his class.

1. _____ Elivira Wanabee traced her ancestry <u>to Snow White</u>.

2. _____ Very few <u>of our clients</u> have complained.

3. _____ Our vice president <u>has installed</u> a hot tub in his office.

4. _____ The tongue is the strongest muscle <u>in the body</u>.

5. _____ You <u>should be enjoying</u> life while you are still old.


Identify the underlined verbal phrases in each of the sentences below by using the following code:

IP   Infinitive phrase      GP   Gerund phrase

PP   Participial phrase

Check your answers at the end of this section.

Examples:  IP  Why do you want <u>to trample my heart</u>?

GP  Yoko hated <u>going to work</u> after her vacation.

PP  A chemistry textbook, <u>hurled by an irate student</u>, got the instructor's attention.

1. _____ <u>Pleased with her progress</u>, Verbena enrolled in an advanced computer course.

2. _____ Tatiana wants <u>to finish her needlework</u> before Gonzalez arrives.

3. _____ Why aren't you here <u>upsetting me</u>?

4. _____ You told me <u>to remind you</u> of the meeting in New Delhi.

5. _____ <u>Planning uprisings</u> was Thor's passion.

6. _____ Three auditors, <u>storming the office</u>, confiscated our records.

7. _____ Our team leader, <u>elated by our success</u>, sent us tickets to the circus.

8. _____ Ollie tried <u>to comfort Primrose</u> when her hamster died.

## The Clause That Refreshes

A **clause** is a group of related words containing a subject and a verb, just as sentences do. Some clauses are **independent** and some are **dependent**.

**Independent Clauses.** An independent clause makes sense by itself and expresses a complete thought. Every simple sentence is an independent clause; however, the term *independent clause* (sometimes called a *main clause*) usually refers to such a group of words as part of a longer sentence.

The scientists were interested in Manuel's research.

The independent clause above is called a simple sentence because it expresses a complete thought and it stands alone.

The scientists were interested in Manuel's research, so they asked him to speak at their next convention.

In the second sentence, *the scientists were interested in Manuel's research* fits the definition of a clause because it has a subject and a predicate, but it does not fit the definition of a sentence because it does not close with end punctuation, and it is part of a longer sentence. *They asked him to speak at their next convention* is also an independent clause. Together these two clauses, joined by *so*, form a single sentence. Therefore, a sentence may consist of a single clause or two or more clauses. Other words that join independent clauses are such words as *and, but, for, therefore, neither* and *nor*.

### ■ EXERCISE FOR PRACTICE

Underline the independent clauses in the following sentences. Check your answers at the end of this section.

Examples:  Phoebe will receive a scholarship but she must pass the state examination.

My doctor gave me three weeks to live; I hope they are in October.

When Jacques missed his flight to France, he spent the night in the airport.

1. Next month Employee Relations will merge with Personnel, which will provide better service for everyone.

2. While we planned the agenda, Glorianna arranged the meeting room.

3. If you are truly objective, you can see that I am right.

4. You can stay on campus, but your dog must find another place to sleep.

5. Let me make you happy or I'll make you miserable.

As a writer you may choose between expressing two closely related ideas as one sentence or as two.

The meeting began on time. Mr. Birch presented an agenda.

or

The meeting began on time and Mr. Birch presented an agenda.

In the first example the two sentences are independent clauses, punctuated as two separate sentences. In the second example, the same two clauses are joined by *and*, and they are part of one sentence.

**NOTE:** For a further review of clauses, see *Clear Writing*, by Diana Bonet, Crisp Publications.

**Dependent Clauses.** A dependent clause has both a subject and a complete verb, but it cannot stand on its own two feet as a sentence—thus the name, *dependent* clause. A dependent clause begins with one of the following words called **subordinating conjunctions**.

while, when, before, where, unless, after, because, though, although, as though, as soon as, until, if, once, as if, since, as, rather than

Another kind of dependent clause begins with a **relative pronoun** such as *that*, *which*, *what*, or *who*.

> We are sorry *that you lost the contract*.

> Frank received a promotion, *which he did not expect*.

> Have you ever met anyone *who was too busy for anything important*?

**Relative clauses** can magically appear in the middle of sentences, as in this example:

> My office partner *who is on vacation* handles the expense vouchers.

This example is two sentences in one:

1. My office partner handles the expense vouchers.
2. He is on vacation.

By changing *He* to *who* you can insert the second sentence easily into the first one.

**NOTE:** If a dependent clause of more than five words comes before the independent clause in the sentence, use a comma after the dependent clause.

> While you were attending the meeting, Harpo finished the financial report.

> If you will bring me the dictionary, I will find the meaning of life.

Generally you do not need a comma if the independent clause comes before the dependent clause.

> Please think about me when I'm gone.

> You will need a resumé once you decide to change jobs.

### ■ EXERCISE FOR PRACTICE

Underline the dependent clause in each sentence below. Check your answers at the end of this section.

Example:  Until the parking lot is paved, you will have to park in the pasture.

Boris updates our instruction manuals regularly because he is our technical editor.

1. Guests who wish to meet the president must stand in the reception line.

2. Things aren't going according to plan, because we never had a plan.

3. If you have doubts about me, you aren't alone.

4. The class schedule, which the staff changed on Thursday, is incorrect.

5. Mr. Flimsy told his staff that he does not tolerate excuses.

6. Since we installed thermal insulation, our heating costs have decreased.

■ **REVIEW EXERCISE**

Identify the underlined clause in each sentence as dependent (**D**), or independent (**I**). Check your answers at the end of this section.

Examples:   _D_  Before you leave the building, please notify the security office.

   _I_  If you have a complaint, please step into the closet.

1. _____ We're planning a sales trip if we can set up some appointments.

2. _____ When Manufacturing completes the back orders, we will send them to you.

3. _____ If you want a place in the sun, prepare to put up with a few blisters. *Dear Abby.*

4. _____ Flavius wrote his letter of resignation, then he threw his chair out the window.

5. _____ Although Junie is fifty-two, she is often mistaken for her daughter.

6. _____ Silvester is someone whom we admire.

7. _____ While she was in Idaho, she visited Sun Valley.

8. _____ My advisor suggested that I enroll in science courses.

9. _____ Experience teaches you to recognize a mistake when you've made it again.

10. _____ You should distrust any job that requires new clothes.

# "Which, and That—Which Is Correct?"

*And it does matter. Use a "which" for a "that" and your readers may have to have their stomachs pumped.*

—Roscoe Born

The **relative pronouns** *which* and *that* often cause confusion for writers. The difference is simple. If the clause is necessary to the meaning of the sentence, use *that*. If the clause is not necessary to the meaning of the sentence, use *which*, then set off the clause with commas.

That: The manual that contains the instructions is on my desk. (It is essential that the instructions are in this particular manual.)

Which: The manual, which contains the instructions, is on my desk. (It is only essential that the manual is on my desk.)

That: Prudence attended a meeting that lasted four hours. (The length of the meeting is important.)

Which: Prudence attended a meeting, which lasted four hours. (The length of the meeting is not as important as the fact that she attended.)

That: The agenda items that are underlined will be discussed first. (Only the items underlined will be discussed first.)

Which: The agenda items, which are underlined, will be discussed first. (All of the agenda items are underlined and they will be discussed before anything else.)

# About Complete Sentences

> *The sentence is a rifle shot, not a buckshot load of facts sprayed in the general direction of the target.*
>
> —Roscoe Born

### From Clauses into Sentences

Now that you know about independent and dependent clauses, you can identify different kinds of sentences by looking at the clauses they contain. There are four kinds of sentences: **simple sentences**, **compound sentences**, **complex sentences**, and **compound-complex sentences**.

1. A **simple sentence** has one independent clause.

   The instructions are confusing.

   A simple sentence can have more than one subject.

   > The *instructions* and the *shipping forms* are confusing.

   A simple sentence can also have more than one verb.

   > The instructions *seemed* easy but *proved* difficult.

   Finally, a simple sentence can have more than one subject and more than one verb.

   > The *instructions* and the *shipping forms seemed* easy to understand, but *proved* difficult to process.

2. A **compound sentence** has at least two independent clauses.

   > I'm right and you're upset.

   > The clock struck twelve, the coach turned into a pumpkin, and the quarterback looked surprised.

3. A **complex sentence** has at least one independent clause and at least one dependent clause. The dependent clause is in *italic* and the independent clause is in **bold**.

   > *As he stepped onto the stage,* **the crowd cheered wildly**.

   > **Butch decided to buy a new copier** *when he heard the cost of the repairs.*

4. A **compound-complex sentence** has at least two independent clauses and at least one dependent clause. Whew! This sentence structure is more complicated than the others, but it isn't difficult to write. Keep these sentences as short as possible. The dependent clauses below are in *italic* and the independent clauses are **bold**.

> *Although I didn't want to be a supervisor,* **I accepted the job**, and **I enjoy it.**

> **Blimpo was very hungry** *since he hadn't eaten all day,* **so he ate the geraniums.**

### ■ EXERCISE FOR PRACTICE

Identify the following sentences as simple (**S**), compound (**CD**), complex (**CX**), or compound-complex (**CDCX**). Check your answers at the end of this section.

Examples:  <u>S</u>  Chang uses the metric system in his work.

<u>CD</u>  Successful organizations act first, then they learn from the results.

<u>CX</u>  I hope to get what I want before I stop wanting it.

<u>CDCX</u>  While Mabel remained stable, Daisy went crazy and John looked wan.

1. _____ Eat dirt, linebacker!

2. _____ You have changed since I've changed.

3. _____ A gentleman is a man who *can* play the accordion, but doesn't.

4. _____ We should take an inventory every six weeks.

5. _____ Miserly Mr. O'Riley and conservative Mr. Cox moaned and groaned over the new budget figures.

6. _____ Since you volunteered, take your time and do it right.

7. _____ My mother had a great deal of trouble with me, but I think she enjoyed it. *Mark Twain*

8. _____ Lightning doesn't strike twice in the same place because the same place isn't there. *Willie Tyler*

9. _____ When I studied for my algebra quiz, I read the wrong notes.

10. _____ Management decided to change the project deadline and to give us more time to complete the job.

# Sentence Bits and Pieces

> *Sign in a British restaurant: Our establishment serves tea in a bag like mother.*

## Fragments

A **sentence fragment** is an incomplete sentence that is punctuated as if it were a real sentence. It is usually missing a subject or a verb. Fragments are awful things. They should be stomped immediately.

FRAGMENT:   I get along well with everybody. Except George and Martha.

SENTENCE:   I get along well with everybody, except George and Martha.

FRAGMENT:   The salesman demonstrated the hardware. While we watched.

SENTENCE:   The salesman demonstrated the hardware while we watched.

FRAGMENT:   I am late. Because I wasn't watching the time.

SENTENCE:   I am late because I wasn't watching the time.

FRAGMENT:   Finding a better solution to the problem. We changed our plan.

SENTENCE:   Finding a better solution to the problem, we changed our plan.

## ■ EXERCISE FOR PRACTICE

Identify the items below as complete sentences (**C**) or sentence fragments (**F**). Check your answers at the end of this section.

Examples:   <u>F</u>  Because travel makes me feel like I'm getting somewhere.

<u>C</u>  Rapunzel is obviously self-disciplined.

<u>F</u>  When the professor entered the data. The system functioned smoothly.

<u>C</u>  I can admit to myself that I am wrong, but I'll never admit it to you. *Ashleigh Brilliant*

1. _____ He needs help. Because he is a dweeb.

2. _____ Students shouldn't eat donuts and peanut butter. Just because they are labeled "lite."

3. _____ Unclear on the concept.

4. _____ The copier is broken. The meeting agendas can't be printed.

5. _____ You are always welcome here. At your own risk.

6. _____ Herkimer completed the reports. Before the deadline.

7. _____ While Maria waited for the meeting to continue, she corrected her notes.

8. _____ When other communication fails, try words.

9. _____ Since Farquar attends five classes a day. He is very busy.

10. _____ Our department is democratic. We do what our manager tells us to do.

## Run-On Sentences

A **run-on sentence** runs on and on. Only correct punctuation can stop a runaway run-on. A run-on sentence contains too much information. It usually contains two complete sentences separated by a comma, or two complete sentences fused beyond recognition. Another name for a run-on sentence is a fused sentence.

> NOT:  Your basil biscuits are delicious they are like little bites of heaven.
>
> YES:  Your basil biscuits are delicious. They are like little bites of heaven.

> NOT:  A storm knocked out the power our computer is down.
>
> YES:  A storm knocked out the power and our computer is down.

> NOT:  The first shift built the assemblers the second shift tested them.
>
> YES:  The first shift built the assemblers; the second shift tested them.

Sometimes writers attempt to correct run-on sentences by inserting a comma between the clauses. This is a bad idea, as it creates another problem called a *comma splice*. The following examples illustrate comma splices and their cures.

> NOT:  Let's hurry, they're not far behind.
>
> YES:  Let's hurry; they're not far behind.
>
> or
>
> Let's hurry, because they're not far behind.
>
> or
>
> Let's hurry! They're not far behind.

NOT:   Someday I'll get my big chance, maybe I've already had it.

YES:   Someday I'll get my big chance; or maybe I've already had it.

NOT:   Lucretia asked her boss for a raise, he said yes.

YES:   Lucretia asked her boss for a raise and he said yes.

NOT:   Every department was on schedule, even Maintenance was on schedule.

YES:   Every department was on schedule, even Maintenance.

## ■ EXERCISE FOR PRACTICE

Identify the items below as complete sentences (**S**) or run-on sentences (**RO**). Run-on sentences include fused sentences and the comma splice. Check your answers at the end of this section.

Examples:   <u>RO</u>   Visual aids should support verbal information, use pictures to enhance your message.

<u>RO</u>   Short sentences are easier to read they are clear and direct.

<u>S</u>   The computer is down. I hope it's something serious. *Stanton Delaplane*

<u>S</u>   Never put off until tomorrow what you can do next week.

1. _____ The day was hot, it made me grouchy.

2. _____ Some writers think that jargon-filled reports sound important. They are wrong.

3. _____ The Forty-Niners won easily they have an excellent quarterback.

4. _____ If you work hard you will succeed.

5. _____ I don't want to bore you, I can't find anyone else to bore.

6. _____ The automatic switch receives its signals from two sources they are located behind the screen.

7. _____ Because the dial was broken, we could not tell that the crystals had vaporized.

8. _____ Our management consultant recommends that we improve our customer service.

9. _____ Forgive me for writing such a long letter I did not have time to write a shorter one.

10. _____ Managers should not substitute rules for personal judgment, they have to trust their employees to make good decisions.

# Parallel Sentences

> *Is sloppy writing caused by ignorance or apathy? I don't know and I don't care.*
>
> —Unknown

Parallel structure means that words, phrases, or clauses in pairs or in a series come from the same grammar groups.

    noun        noun
*Ichabod* and *Petunia* were promoted.

             gerund phrase       gerund phrase
Ophelia enjoys *taking minutes* and *transcribing them.*

    independent clause       independent clause
*History will be kind to me;* for *I intend to write it.* Winston Churchill.

If more items were added to the examples above, they would have to be part of the same grammar groups as well.

Parallel structure is second nature to a good writer. Readers expect balance and order, and they become annoyed when they have to cope with something like this:

Sluggo O'Malley likes to sing, to waltz, and mud wrestling.

If you want to mend this faulty parallel structure, you can change the sentence to something like this:

Sluggo O'Malley likes to sing, to waltz, and to mud wrestle.

or

Sluggo O'Malley likes singing, waltzing, and mud wrestling.

## ■ EXERCISE FOR PRACTICE

1. Identify the sentences below as parallel (**P**) or not parallel (**NP**).

2. Correct the sentences that are not parallel on the lines provided. You are likely to find more than one way to correct the sentences that are parallel. Check possible answers at the end of this section.

Examples:    NP    A quality awareness program requires not only employee involvement but also that managers be leaders.

A quality awareness program requires not only employee involvement but also management leadership.

NP    We could not decide whether to organize a car pool or letting employees find rides for themselves.

We could not decide whether to organize a car pool or to let employees find rides for themselves.

P    Blondie is talented, willful, and rich.

1. _____ Maryloubeth decided to edit her report and that she would write a memo to her manager.

2. _____ I came, I saw, I conquered.

3. _____ Riding the train is less expensive than to drive a car.

4. _____ Hung Ly was shy, quiet, and a gentle man.

5. _____ The new system is too complex, too expensive, and too risky.

6. _____ Nothing is impossible if you don't have to do it yourself.

7. _____ Our office needs new carpets, fresh paint, and to be given a good cleaning.

8. _____ Miss Anthrope thanked her students for being prepared and promptness.

_____

9. _____ Our engineers plan to build a bridge that will last—at least until construction is complete.

_____

10. _____ Environmental issues are of critical concern to scientists, to business professionals, to government officials, and every citizen should be concerned as well.

_____

_____

If your writing sounds bumpy or confusing to you, it will sound that way to your reader as well. Be objective. You can remedy problems with nonparallel sentences by writing short sentences or by matching grammar groups—by matching nouns with nouns, phrases with phrases, and so forth. Always make it your goal to write clear sentences that express your meaning instantly and unmistakably.

Also, you can combat nonparallel construction by using your ears as well as your eyes. Read your writing aloud and listen for a smooth flow. The sweet sound of a well-written sentence provides as much reliable feedback as does your knowledge of good grammar.

## Answers for Section II

Page 82

1. Ezra pounded his fists on the desk.

2. One partridge and two pear trees disappeared from the Christmas inventory.

3. Our new accountant has more dollars than sense.

4. Ziggy bought a new car last night and hit a police van this morning.

5. Aliens visited the school library and the administration office.

Page 82

1. By the end of the week our tired team completed the demanding project.

2. <u>Bimbo and Bimbette, the Branson twins,</u> <u>live in a make-believe world.</u>

3. <u>Wild horses</u> <u>couldn't make me bungee jump.</u>

4. <u>I</u> <u>studied for the quiz for six hours.</u>

5. <u>Managers who support their employees' professional growth</u> <u>are good mentors.</u>

## Page 83

1. <u>IMP</u>  You must pay the rent.

2. <u>INT</u>  Is that the new accountant who is counting beans at his desk?

3. <u>D</u>  Let's discuss my problem.

4. <u>E</u>  Forget it!

5. <u>D</u>  To write is not simple.

6. <u>INT</u>  What shall I do until you change your bad habits?

7. <u>IMP</u>  Come in and eat before we both starve! (Sign in restaurant window)

8. <u>E</u>  No way!

## Page 86

1. <u>PP</u>  Elvira Wanabee traced her ancestry <u>to Snow White.</u>

2. <u>PP</u>  Very few <u>of our clients</u> have complained.

3. <u>VP</u>  Our vice president <u>has installed</u> a hot tub in his office.

4. <u>PP</u>  The tongue is the strongest muscle <u>in the body.</u>

5. <u>VP</u>  You <u>should be enjoying</u> life while you are still old.

## Page 87

1. <u>PP</u>  <u>Pleased with her progress,</u> Verbena enrolled in an advanced computer course.

2. <u>IP</u>  Tatiana wants <u>to finish her needlework</u> before Gonzalez arrives.

3. <u>GP</u>  Why aren't you here <u>upsetting me?</u>

4. <u>IP</u>  You told me <u>to remind you</u> of the meeting in New Delhi.

5. <u>GP</u>  <u>Planning uprisings</u> was Thor's passion.

6.  <u>PP</u>  Three auditors, <u>storming the office,</u> confiscated our records.

7.  <u>PP</u>  Our team leader, <u>elated by our success,</u> sent us tickets to the circus.

8.  <u>IP</u>  Ollie tried <u>to comfort Primrose</u> when her hamster died.

### Page 88

1.  <u>Next month Employee Relations will merge with Personnel,</u> which will provide better service for everyone.

2.  While we planned the agenda, <u>Glorianna arranged the meeting room.</u>

3.  If you are truly objective, <u>you can see</u> that I am right.

4.  <u>You can stay on campus,</u> but <u>your dog must find another place to sleep.</u>

5.  <u>Let me make you happy</u> or <u>I'll make you miserable.</u>

### Page 90

1.  Guests <u>who wish to meet the president</u> must stand in the reception line.

2.  Things aren't going according to plan, <u>because we never had a plan.</u>

3.  If <u>you have doubts about me,</u> you aren't alone.

4.  The class schedule, <u>which the staff changed on Thursday,</u> is incorrect.

5.  Mr. Flimsy told his staff <u>that he does not tolerate excuses.</u>

6.  <u>Since we installed thermal insulation,</u> our heating costs have decreased.

### Page 90

1.  <u>D</u>  We're planning a sales trip <u>if we can set up some appointments.</u>

2.  <u>I</u>  When Manufacturing completes the back orders <u>we will send them to you.</u>

3.  <u>I</u>  If you want a place in the sun, <u>prepare to put up with a few blisters.</u>
    *Dear Abby.*

4.  <u>D</u>  Flavius wrote his letter of resignation, <u>then he threw his chair out the window.</u>

5.  <u>D</u>  Although Junie is fifty-two, she is often mistaken for her daughter.

6.  <u>D</u>  Silvester is someone <u>whom we admire.</u>

7.  <u>I</u>  While she was in Idaho, <u>she visited Sun Valley.</u>

8. __D__ My advisor suggested <u>that I enroll in science courses.</u>

9. __I__ Experience teaches you to recognize a mistake when you've made it again.

10. __I__ <u>You should distrust any job</u> that requires new clothes.

## Page 93

1. __S__ Eat dirt, linebacker!

2. __CX__ You have changed since I've changed.

3. __CX__ A gentleman is a man who *can* play the accordion, but doesn't.

4. __S__ We should take an inventory every six weeks.

5. __S__ Miserly Mr. O'Riley and conservative Mr. Cox moaned and groaned over the new budget figures.

6. __CDCX__ Since you volunteered, take your time and do it right.

7. __CD__ My mother had a great deal of trouble with me, but I think she enjoyed it. *Mark Twain*

8. __CX__ Lightning doesn't strike twice in the same place because the same place isn't there. *Willie Tyler*

9. __CX__ When I studied for my algebra quiz, I read the wrong notes.

10. __S__ Management decided to change the project deadline and to give us more time to complete the job.

## Page 94

1. __F__ He needs help. Because he is a dweeb.

2. __F__ Students shouldn't eat donuts and peanut butter. Just because they are labeled "lite."

3. __F__ Unclear on the concept.

4. __S__ The copier is broken. The meeting agendas can't be printed.

5. __F__ You are always welcome here. At your own risk.

6. __F__ Herkimer completed the reports. Before the deadline.

7. __S__ While Maria waited for the meeting to continue, she corrected her notes.

8.  S  When other communication fails, try words.

9.  F  Since Farquar attends five classes a day. He is very busy.

10. S  Our department is democratic. We do what our manager tells us to do.

## Page 96

1.  RO  The day was hot, it made me grouchy.

2.  S  Some writers think that jargon-filled reports sound important. They are wrong.

3.  RO  The Forty-Niners won easily they have an excellent quarterback.

4.  S  If you work hard you will succeed.

5.  RO  I don't want to bore you, I can't find anyone else to bore.

6.  RO  The automatic switch receives its signals from two sources they are located behind the screen.

7.  S  Because the dial was broken, we could not tell that the crystals had vaporized.

8.  S  Our management consultant recommends that we improve our customer service.

9.  RO  Forgive me for writing such a long letter I did not have time to write a shorter one.

10. RO  Managers should not substitute rules for personal judgment, they have to trust their employees to make good decisions.

## Page 98

1.  NP  Maryloubeth decided to edit her report and that she would write a memo to her manager.

   *Maryloubeth decided to edit her report and to write a memo to her manager.*

2.  P  I came, I saw, I conquered.

   *OK*

3. __NP__   Riding the train is less expensive than to drive a car.

*Riding the train is less expensive than driving a car.*

4. __NP__   Hung Ly was shy, quiet, and a gentle man.

*Hung Ly was shy, quiet, and gentle.*

5. __P__   The new system is too complex, too expensive, and too risky.

*OK*

6. __P__   Nothing is impossible if you don't have to do it yourself.

*OK*

7. __NP__   Our office needs new carpets, fresh paint, and to be given a good cleaning.

*Our office needs new carpets, fresh paint, and a good cleaning.*

8. __NP__   Miss Anthrope thanked her students for being prepared and promptness.

*Miss Anthrope thanked her students for being prepared and prompt.*

9. __P__   Our engineers plan to build a bridge that will last—at least until construction is complete.

*OK*

10. __NP__   Environmental issues are of critical concern to scientists, to business professionals, to government officials, and every citizen should be concerned as well.

*Environmental issues are of critical concern to scientists, to business professionals, to government officials, and to every citizen.*

# *Chapter* III

# Using Words Effectively

## Using Words Effectively

> *Just say NO to cliches.*

This section is about using the right words to communicate your ideas. Learning to use words correctly means that you are using Standard English, which is the generally accepted expression of educated people. You do not need a college education in order to use Standard English. Begin with this book. Study the rules. Do the practice exercises. Listen to good speech. Read good literature. Then gradually change your speaking and writing habits by setting goals and making a sustained effort. Actively ask for help, and always give yourself credit for your progress. Remember that changing habits is a *conscious* choice.

## Tricky Words

> *English is funny. A fat chance and a slim chance means the same thing.*
> —Unknown

Here are some tricky words that are often misused and abused. Frequently, we confuse them with other words they resemble. Some of these words are considered nonstandard, or illiterate; therefore, they are unsuitable for writing or speaking in business situations. These "grammar goblins" should be avoided. However, some words haunt even the experts, and they don't always agree on which words are acceptable. If you are in doubt, consult a good dictionary.

**accept - except**

*Accept* (verb) means "to receive": I *accept* your not-so-humble apology.

*Except* (usually a preposition) means "to leave out or to exclude": Everyone wants to change the world, *except* Waldo.

**NOTE:** *Except* is occasionally a verb meaning "to exclude": Please *except* me from your "Most Promising Employee" list.

## affect - effect

*Affect* (verb) means "to influence": Yuan's decision *affected* everyone.

*Effect* (noun) means "a result": What is the *effect* of the new "Whitewash Policy"?

**NOTE:** Less frequently, *affect* (verb) means "to put on": Mabel Rose *affected* a hoity-toity English accent. *Effect* (verb) means "to achieve" or "to bring about": The team *effected* a workable solution.

## all ready - already

*All ready* (adjective phrase) means "everyone or everything is ready": We are *all ready* to begin the immortality experiment. You may be able to omit the word *all* in some cases: We are *ready* to begin the immortality experiment.

*Already* (abverb) means "previously": Tatiana has left *already*.

**NOTE:** *Already* is used as slang in this sentence: What do you want *already*?

## amount - number

*Amount* (noun) denotes quantity, or things in bulk or mass: No *amount* of money could buy her heart.

*Number* (noun) involves objects that can be counted: A *number* of diners offered a toast to white bread.

## awful - awfully

*Awful* (adjective) is colloquial when it is used to mean "ugly, very bad, or offensive": Her table manners were shocking. (not *awful*)

In Formal English *awful* is an adjective meaning "awe-inspiring," although it is seldom used in that form: The double rainbow was *awful*.

*Awfully* (adverb) is used in the colloquial sense to mean "very": I am *awfully* tired. Use *very* instead. Avoid *awful* and *awfully* in Formal writing and speech, unless you mean "awe-inspiring." Both are acceptable in casual speech.

## between - among

*Between* (preposition) refers to two persons, objects, or ideas: Divide the spoils *between* Og and Thor.

*Among* (preposition) implies three or more: I love wandering *among* the bookshelves.

**NOTE:** *Amongst* is also correct, but it is used more widely in England than in the United States.

### bring - take

*Bring* (verb) means "to come here with": *Bring* the chainsaw to me.

*Take* (verb) means "to go there with": *Take* the chainsaw to the nice man.

### cannot - can not

*Cannot* is the correct form, by popular demand.

### data - datum

*Data* is the plural form of *datum:* These are the *data* that you requested. In English, *data* has gained wide acceptance as a singular noun, especially when it refers to a body of information: We lost all of the *data* in the computer.

Acceptable: These *data* are reliable. *or* This *data* is reliable.

### farther - further

*Farther* (adverb) refers to measured distance: Cleese drove *farther* into the forest.

*Further* (adverb) means "to a greater physical degree or quantity": The committee considered the proposal *further*. In Informal English these words are used interchangeably without raising too many eyebrows. However, a distinction does exist in Formal English, so put this information in your "Good to Know" file.

### fewer - less

*Fewer* is used only when something is actually counted: We have *fewer* staff assistants than we had last year.

*Less* refers to quantity: We experienced *less* turnover this year.

**NOTE:** In recent years, *fewer* is declining in use and *less* is taking its place—more and more: We need three *less* chairs at the conference table.

### imply - infer

*Imply* (verb) means "to suggest or state directly": Samuel *implied* that we would be a better team if we did things his way.

*Infer* means "to draw a conclusion": Joe *inferred* from the letter that he was a hero.

A writer or speaker *implies*; a reader or a listener *infers*. To be correct and confident, you should know the difference between these two words, even though they are often used interchangeably.

### lend - loan

*Lend* is a verb: Please *lend* us a hand.

*Loan* is a noun: If we can get a *loan* from the bank, we can stay in business.

### loose - lose

*Loose* (adjective) means "free." The *loose* goose chased the moose from Talouse.

*Lose* (verb) is the opposite of win. It rhymes with *news*: Please help me *lose* those "Lonesome Polecat Blues."

### may - can

*May* (verb) means "to have permission": *May* I have this waltz? It also suggests possibility: We *may* yet have time to save the planet.

*Can* (verb) means "to be able": *Can* you learn to enjoy doing something badly when you can't do it well? These words are used interchangeably in Standard English, although *can* is used more often.

### precede - proceed

*Precede* (verb) means "to go before": May *precedes* June.

*Proceed* (verb) means "to go forward": We should *proceed* with the interview.

### principal - principle

*Principal* (noun) means "chief," "the head of a school," or "the main point": The *principal* on our investment is $12,000. The *principal* of Hoorah High School is Mrs. Applegate.

*Principal* (adjective) means "main" or "most important": Our *principal* guideline is to treat our employees fairly.

*Principle* (noun) means "a rule," "a truth," or "a code of behavior": The Ten Commandments are religious *principles*. (Remember: principLE = ruLE)

### their - there

*Their* (possessive pronoun) shows ownership: This is *their* plan for expansion. (Remember: tHEIR = one who owns something)

*There* (adverb) refers to a place: Put the dragon over *there*. (Remember: tHERE = HERE, which is the opposite of tHERE)

*There* is also an expletive (an introductory word): *There* is a seasoning for everything.

### ■ EXERCISE FOR PRACTICE

Underline the correct word in the following sentences. Check your answers at the end of this section.

Examples:  I **(imply, _infer_)** from your call that you are ready to negotiate.

The stock clerk withdrew a **(_number_, amount)** of articles from the inventory.

1. Shall we **(bring, take)** the albatross with us?
2. Did you **(loose, lose)** your marbles in the dark?
3. **(There, Their)** is no substitute for a genuine lack of preparation.
4. When **(principles, principals)** fail, try thinking.
5. **(Can, May)** we please leave at 5:00?
6. I think that I **(can, may)** finish the report on time.
7. We plan to **(precede, proceed)** with the expansion of the manufacturing plant.
8. Ting Chau analyzed the **(data, datum)** in the files.
9. Felix, Peewee, and Celeste argued **(among, between)** themselves.
10. Please **(accept, except)** the fact that most of my faults aren't my fault.

## Tacky Words

> *Do not write in a manner that would annoy you if you had to read it. Likewise, do not speak in a manner that would offend you if you had to listen to it.*
> —Diana Bonet

The following words and phrases have crept slowly into English usage. Although they are probably permanent fixtures, they are considered nonstandard and you should avoid them, especially in writing. You may be surprised to find that some of these words do not even exist in English (anyways, alright).

### ain't

Yes, *ain't* is in the dictionary, as is the word *yackety-yack*, because the dictionary simply includes words that people use. In the dictionary *ain't* is defined as ''nonstandard.'' Educated speakers are particularly opposed to *ain't*, so please don't use it, because you are going to upset a lot of people if you do. To break yourself of the *ain't* habit, try replacing it with *yackety-yack*.

### alot

You will not find this word in the dictionary, although it has been seen a lot lately. In fact, *alot* is not one word, but two words (*a lot*). Look for a substitute or omit it, as it is considered nonstandard English.

> NOT: I enjoyed the presentation a lot.
>
> OK: I enjoyed the presentation very much.
>
> or
>
> BETTER: The presentation was excellent.
>
> NOT: Her alibi sounds like a lot of baloney to me.
>
> YES: Her alibi sounds like baloney to me.

### being as how

This phrase is nonstandard. Try *because*.

> NOT: Being as how we are late, let's play hooky.
>
> YES: Because we are late, let's play hooky.

### busted

Try *broke* or *burst*. *Busted* is a nonstandard form of *burst*, as *cuss* is a nonstandard form of *curse*.

NOT:     The pipe busted.

YES:     The pipe burst.

NOT:     My computer is busted.

YES:     My computer is broken.

## can't hardly

This is a double negative. Leave out *hardly*.

NOT:     I can't hardly hear you.

YES:     Speak up!

or

I can't hear you very well.

or

I am having trouble hearing you.

## don't got

This one is easy. Change *got* to *have*. The word *got* is a weak verb. You can usually replace it with a better word.

NOT:     I don't got the time.

YES:     I don't have the time.

NOT:     They got a loan to start their new business.

YES:     They received a loan to start their new business.

## etc.

*Etc.* is an abbreviation of the Latin words *et cetera*. In English it means "and other things." Some say that using *etc.* at the end of a list is a lazy writing practice. Use *and other* or *and so forth*. Also, you can rephrase the sentence to avoid the problem.

NOT AS GOOD:     Jules prefers Beethoven, Mozart, and so forth.

BETTER:     Jules prefers composers such as Beethoven and Mozart.

Always avoid *and etc.*; it is redundant.

**had better**

Substitute *should*.

> NOT:  You had better write your memoirs.
>
> YES:  You should write your memoirs.

**hisself**

This is not a real word. The correct word is *himself.*

> NOT:  Barney tripped hisself on the rope.
>
> YES:  Barney tripped himself on the rope.

**irregardless**

There is no such word as *irregardless*. Use *regardless*.

> NOT:  Irregardless of your opinion, Chicken Little only has to be right once.
>
> YES:  Regardless of your opinion, Chicken Little only has to be right once.

**kind of a / sort of a**

Omit *a*. Give us some *kind of* proposal by Wednesday. Now that we have eliminated the *a*, let's eliminate *kind of* and *sort of* entirely, when we mean *somewhat*. Be specific. *Kind of* and *sort of* sound wishy-washy (indecisive), and they are nonstandard. If you can't be definite, choose another word.

> NOT:  Success hasn't spoiled me; I've always been kind of a pain.
>
> YES:  Success hasn't spoiled me; I've always been a pain.

> NOT:  I find people somewhat interesting, but I've never liked them.
>
> YES:  People are mildly interesting, but I've never liked them.

**like**

Eliminate this word unless you are making a comparison.

> NOT:  Then I caught like this really big wave.
>
> YES:  Then I caught an enormous wave.
>
> YES:  My love is like a red rose. (comparison)

## really

This is a conversational cliché. Outgrow the use of *really* as an adverb modifying an adjective. It's cute, but not effective. Really!

NOT:     Then I got this really big bonus for Christmas.

YES:     Then I received a large bonus for Christmas.

This word is pronounced ''reel-ee,'' rather than ''rul-lee.''

## the reason is because

This expression is redundant. Use *because*.

NOT:     Talk is cheap. The reason is because supply exceeds demand.

YES:     Talk is cheap because supply exceeds demand.

## relate to

This phrase is yuppie slang, which gives it an ''in'' quality; however, it is not accurate when you mean *to understand* or *to share the same experience.*

NOT:     I can relate to your ideas about the environment.

YES:     I understand (share) your ideas about the environment.

## somewheres / nowheres / anywheres

These words are nonexistent, but persistent. Please remove the ''esses'';
*somewhere, nowhere, anywhere.*

NOT:     I know I put my gerbil somewheres; he is nowheres to be found; if you see him anywheres, send him home.

YES:     I know I put my gerbil somewhere; he is nowhere to be found; if you see him anywhere, send him home.

## try and / sure and

These should be *try to* and *sure to.*

NOT:     Try and do something at once, rather than everything at once.

YES:     Try to do something at once, rather than everything at once.

NOT:   Be sure and send me a fax.

YES:   Be sure to send me a fax.

**used to could**

Omit *could*.

NOT:   We used to could send deliveries directly to New Mexico.

YES:   We used to send deliveries directly to New Mexico.

After the verb *did*, say *use to* (omit the *d*). Didn't you use to have a beard?

**went and / take and**

These are redundant expressions.

NOT:   Take and drive me to the airport.

YES:   Drive me to the airport.

NOT:   Sammy went and did his homework.

YES:   Sammy did his homework.

**where**

Don't use *where* when you mean *that*.

NOT:   I saw where you won the lottery.

YES:   I saw that you won the lottery.

**worst way**

This is a colloquial expression meaning *badly*.

NOT:   I wanted the promotion in the worst way.

YES:   I wanted the promotion badly.

### Other Tacky Words to Tackle

**How come?**  Use *why:* Why aren't you leaving?

**till**     Use *until. Till* means to plow the soil. Stay until tomorrow.

**all of a sudden** Use *suddenly;* it's shorter. Suddenly we saw daylight.

**this**     Use *a* or *an* in front of a noun. There was a (not *this*) juggler.

**took off**   Use *ran.* Suddenly Bingo ran (not *took off*) into the street.

**started to**   Use *began to* or another verb. Hallie began to ask about the quiz. OR Hallie asked about the quiz.

### ■ EXERCISE FOR PRACTICE

Rewrite or change the following sentences to reflect Standard English usage. Check possible answers at the end of this section.

Examples: I ain't done no harm.

     I haven't harmed anyone.

     We can't hardly do anything without including Bob.

     We can't do much without including Bob.

1. The extra printer paper is somewheres on my desk.
2. The pizza won't be here till 7:00.
3. We put alot of extra time into the project.
4. Three pipes busted in the basement.
5. Irregardless of others' advice, make only big mistakes.
6. Blessed are the inept, the slothful, the bored, etc.
7. How come you went and left me with the sharks?
8. We have like three weeks to finish the project.
9. Barton cut hisself with his new razor.
10. I can really relate to your story.

# Sticky Words

*Writing is easy. All you have to do is cross out the wrong words.*
—Mark Twain

Some words always seem to be problems. When do you use *I - me, lie - lay, sit - set, to - too - two,* and *who - whom*? Here is a review of most of the words that continually create confusion in English. Think of this review as mental glue. Perhaps, this time, these words will stick in your mind correctly.

### I - me / we - us / who - whom

These sets of words are presented together because each of them is handled in the same way. On page 15 you will find a list of pronouns. Notice that *I, we,* and *who* are in the "Subject" column and *me, us,* and *whom* are in the "Object" column. Therefore, *I, we,* and *who* are used as subjects of sentences, and *me, us,* and *whom* are used as objects (direct objects, indirect objects, or objects of prepositions). Place a check mark next to those sentences that sound correct.

_____ I need your access code.

_____ Me needs your access code.

_____ We like aardvarks.

_____ Us likes aardvarks.

_____ Who is calling, please?

_____ Whom is calling, please?

In each set of examples you should have checked the first sentence. Let's look at each part separately.

### I - me

The word *I* is the correct subject of the first sentence. *I* can be used as a subject, but not as an object. In the sentence *It is I,* the word *I* is correct, because it renames the subject, *It. I* is called a **predicate nominative**.

The second sentence, *Me needs your access code*, sounds like baby talk, except that few babies know about access codes. *Me* cannot be used as the subject of a sentence, because it is always used as an object, as in the sentence: Billy asked *me* to cook his goose. *Me* is the **direct object**.

Another kind of object is an **object of a preposition**. Review Section I briefly for a quick refresher on prepositions. *Me* is used as an object of a preposition. The word *between* is a preposition; therefore, *between you and me* is correct. The following sentences are examples of *me* as the object of a preposition:

> Fireflies lit the night for Pansy and me.

> To Sybil and me, the plan seemed irresponsible.

> Just between you and me, some things have to be believed to be seen.

**we - us**

Which sentence is correct?

> Management gave *us* secretaries a 20 percent pay raise.

> Management gave *we* secretaries a 15 percent pay raise.

If you said the first sentence, you are correct . . . and you would receive a larger pay raise. If you are unsure about *we* and *us*, remove the *secretaries*: Management gave *us* a 20 percent pay raise. As with *I - me*, use *we* as a subject and *us* as an object.

> Subject: *We* cannot think clearly with clenched fists.

> Object: People ask *us* dumb questions for a reason.

**who - whom**

You don't have to be a rocket scientist to use *who* and *whom* correctly. If butlers in old English movies can do it, so can you. *Who* is also in the subject column on page 15. Always remember these two facts about *who*: (1) It is used only to refer to people; and (2) it is always used as a subject (or a predicate nominative).

> NOT: The cat we fed is the one *who* purrs constantly.

> YES: The cat we fed is the one *that* purrs constantly.

> NOT: *Whom* asked for the transfer?

> YES: *Who* asked for the transfer?

NOT: *Whom* do you think I am?

YES: *Who* do you think I am?

*Whom* is used as an object.

NOT: Is this the person to *who* I am speaking?

YES: Is this the person to *whom* I am speaking?

NOT: *Who* did you send to the meeting? (*You* is the subject.)

YES: *Whom* did you send to the meeting? (*Whom* is the direct object.)

## lie - lay

For real confidence with these sticky verbs, begin by memorizing the tense of each verb. Make up sentences and practice them until they sound right.

| Present | Past | Past Participle |
| --- | --- | --- |
| lie | lay | had lain |
| lay | laid | had laid |

*To lie* means "to recline." A second definition of *lie* is to tell a humongous fib. This definition isn't the one that causes trouble, except for the person telling the falsehood. It is the "reclining" *lie* that causes concern. The verb *to lie* is **intransitive**, which means it does not take a direct object.

> *Lie* down and rest your busy bones. (*Down* is an adverb, not a direct object.)

*To lay* means to put or place something. The "something" that is placed is a direct object, so *to lay* is always a **transitive verb**. It requires a direct object: *Lay* the diskette on the desk.

NOT: *Laying* in the sun is bad for your skin.

YES: *Lying* in the sun is bad for your skin.

NOT: Now I *lie* me down to sleep.

YES: Now I *lay* me down to sleep.

NOT:    Sterling *had laid* on the deck all day.

YES:    Sterling *had lain* on the deck all day.

NOT:    *Have* you *lain* the ground rules for the final exams?

YES:    *Have* you *laid* the ground rules for the final exams?

## to - too - two

*To* means *toward*. It is a **preposition**.

Montana road sign: *Go to Helena!*

*To* is also the first word of the **infinitive form of a verb**.

Julio's goal in life is *to* be a bad example.

*Too* means "also."

Gypsy Sue wants to be a bad example *too.*

*Too* also means "excessively."

I prefer Twinkies because Pop Tarts require *too* much cooking.

*Two* is the number 2. 1 + 1 = 2.

## ■ EXERCISE FOR PRACTICE

In the following exercise, underline the correct word choice in each sentence. Check your answers at the end of this section.

Examples:    I am **(to, two, <u>too</u>)** old **(<u>to</u>, too, two)** run one marathon, much less **(<u>two</u>, to, too)**.

**(<u>Who</u>, whom)** is taking the minutes of the meeting?

**(<u>Zonkers and I</u>, Zonkers and me)** agree that the secret to life is to keep breathing.

1. **(Who, Whom)** did you ask to plan the conference?

2. Zoie wrote a thank-you poem to **(Adolf and I, Adolf and me)**.

3. We would like **(to, too)** install **(too, two)** phones in our office **(to, too)**.

4. Yesterday the order forms were **(lying, laying)** on the counter.

5. In business and in chess, the winner is the one **(who, whom)** makes the last mistake.

6. Nervously, Patty Putz **(lay, laid)** her hand on the thousand-dollar bill.

7. Please do **(we, us)** programmers a favor: if it doesn't work, try jumper cables.

8. For **(who, whom)** is the phone message?

9. Hecuba and **(he, him)** believe that horsepower was better when only horses had it.

10. Hershel's proposal sounds **(too, to, two)** good **(too, to, two)** be true.

# Wacky Words

> *He spoke with a certain what-is-it in his voice, and I could see that if not actually disgruntled, he was far from being gruntled.*
>
> —P. G. Wodehouse

You will *hear* wacky words more than you will see them. These are words that are confused and abused in pronunciation, and sometimes in spelling. Following is a list of wacky words that are often mispronounced. Because we hear them spoken incorrectly so often, the wrong way sounds right. Be careful not to become ''fossilized'' so that you no longer hear incorrect pronunciation. Untoungle your tang, unlazy your lips, and proceed with proper pronunciation. In the spaces below, check those that you routinely pronounce correctly. Then begin working on the others with the help of a friend.

|    | Word | Correct Pronunciation | Mispronunciation |
|----|------|----------------------|------------------|
| 1. _____ | ask | ask | ax |
| 2. _____ | athlete | ATH-leet | ATH-uh-leet |
| 3. _____ | burglar | BER-gler | BER-guh-ler |
| 4. _____ | children | CHIL-dren | CHIL-dern |
| 5. _____ | column | COL-um | COL-yum |
| 6. _____ | creek | creek | crick |

| | Word | Correct Pronunciation | Mispronunciation |
|---|---|---|---|
| 7. _____ | directory | di-REC-tor-ee | dir-REC-tree |
| 8. _____ | environment | en-VI-ron-ment | en-VI-ern-mint |
| 9. _____ | Arab | ARR-ub | Ay-rab |
| 10. _____ | February | FEB-ru-a-ry | Feb-u-AIR-ee |
| 11. _____ | genuine | JEN-you-in | jen-you-WINE |
| 12. _____ | height | hite | hite-th |
| 13. _____ | hundred | HUN-dred | HUN-dert |
| 14. _____ | idea | i-DEE-uh | i-DEER |
| 15. _____ | library | LIE-brer-ee | LIE-bare-ee |
| 16. _____ | nuclear | NEW-clee-ar | NEW-que-lar |
| 17. _____ | realtor | REE-al-tor | ree-LA-tor |
| 18. _____ | roof | roof | ruff |
| 19. _____ | silicon | sil-i-CON | sil-i-CONE |

## RUNTOGETHERSENTENCES

Words become double-wacky when we run together entire sentences. Good communication means clear, distinct speech. To speak clearly, **enunciate.** To practice separating words and pronouncing words distinctly, wrap your mouth around the sentences in the exercise below.

## ■ EXERCISE FOR PRACTICE

Write out what you think the following run-together words mean; then say each corrected sentence slowly and clearly. Check at the end of this section for a "translation."

1. Dyaevr seeim? _____

2. Howvyabin? _____

3. Dyunnerstan? _____

4. Whachadoon? _____

5. I toljuhthousantimz. _____

6. I heardjuh. _____

7. I roetchalassmunt. _____

8. Woodjagimmesom? _____

9. Jeetchet? _____

10. Jawannadans? _____

# Answers for Section III

## TRICKY WORDS

Page 111

1. take.  2. lose.  3. There.  4. principles.  5. May.  6. can.  7. proceed.
8. data.  9. among.  10. accept.

## TACKY WORDS

Page 117

(Possible answers)

1. The extra printer paper is somewhere on my desk.

OR

The extra printer paper is on my desk.

2. The pizza won't be here until 7:00.

3. We put a lot of extra time into the project.

OR

We put extra time into the project.

4. Three pipes burst in the basement.

5. Regardless of others' advice, make only big mistakes.

6. Blessed are the inept, the slothful, the bored, and so forth.

OR

Blessed are the inept, the slothful, and the bored.

7. Why did you leave me with the sharks?

8. We have three weeks to finish the project. (omit *like*)

9. Barton cut himself with his new razor.

10. I empathize with your story.

OR

I certainly understand your story.


## STICKY WORDS

Page 121

1. Whom.   2. Adolf and me.   3. to, two, too.   4. lying.   5. who.   6. laid   7. us.
8. whom.   9. he.   10. too, to.

Page 123

1. Do you ever see him?

2. How have you been?

3. Do you understand?

4. What are you doing?

5. I told you a thousand times.

6. I heard you.

7. I wrote to you last month.

8. Would you give me some?

9. Have you eaten yet? NOT: Did you eat yet?

10. Do you want to dance?

# Chapter *IV*

# Spelling, Punctuation, and Capitalization

# Laffing at Mispelled Words

*English spelling is the world's most awesome mess.*
— Mario Pei

The following words are spelling demons that can make you shout "Enuf!" Study those that give you trouble and practice writing them. To make spelling fun, conduct an old-fashioned spelling bee with friends and family. With a little time and attention, these words do not have to be problems.

| | | | | |
|---|---|---|---|---|
| ache | character | does | heard | ninety |
| absence | choose | early | height | ninth |
| accommodate | committee | eighth | hoping | often |
| achieve | competent | embarrass | hour | occasionally |
| acquaint | condemn | enough | instead | occurred |
| acquire | conscious | excellent | knew | omission |
| acquit | courteous | existence | knowledge | omitted |
| across | criticize | familiar | laughing | opinion |
| again | curious | February | loose | opportunity |
| aggressive | deceive | finally | lose | parallel |
| amateur | definite | foreign | maintenance | perceive |
| answer | describe | forfeit | management | permanent |
| anxious | description | forty | maneuver | persistent |
| apparent | desirable | friend | mathematics | piece |
| argument | desperate | fulfill | meant | possess |
| article | develop | government | minute | preceding |
| athlete | disappear | grammar | mischievous | prejudice |
| beginning | disappoint | guarantee | misspelled | prevalent |
| believe | discipline | guess | necessary | privilege |
| business | dilemma | half | niece | procedure |

| proceed | sacrifice | sincerely | there | villain |
|---------|-----------|-----------|-------|---------|
| professor | schedule | sophomore | though | where |
| pursue | seize | straight | through | whether |
| raise | sense | strength | truly | which |
| receive | separate | surprise | twelfth | whole |
| recommend | shining | synonym | unusual | would |
| rhythm | similar | their | vacuum | |

*FRANK & ERNEST reprinted by permission of NEA, Inc.*

*Bad spellers of the world, untie!*

# Punctuation? Of Course!

> *A well-written sentence almost punctuates itself.*
> —Wilson Follett

Punctuation marks are the traffic cops of writing. They tell you when to slow down, pause, stop, and continue. Perhaps you have seen the following sentence, which illustrates the need for proper punctuation. How would you punctuate this sentence? Try it, then check your answer at the bottom of the page.*

What is is what is not is not is it not

Since punctuation is so important in writing, this section reviews the rules that you need most often to help you write well. Punctuation rules apply to writing only, as we punctuate speech with our voices, with pauses, and with body language. Let's review the most important rules for **end punctuation, commas, and semicolons.**

## ■ EXERCISE FOR PRACTICE

As a review, place the proper punctuation mark next to its name. Check your answers at the end of this section.

| | |
|---|---|
| 1. Period | 7. Dash |
| 2. Exclamation mark | 8. Parenthesis |
| 3. Question mark | 9. Apostrophe |
| 4. Comma | 10. Hyphen |
| 5. Semicolon | 11. Quotation marks |
| 6. Colon | 12. Elipses |

*What is, is; what is not, is not; is it not?

Over the years, punctuation in writing has relaxed, and in some cases disappeared entirely. Of the 12 punctuation marks in the previous practice exercise, you need only two of them regularly—the comma and the period. You could probably write a dozen letters or memos and never need a semicolon.

Here is the queen of punctuation rules: **DO NOT OVERPUNCTUATE.** This rule simplifies the muddle of problems with punctuation. This rule, however, does *not* apply to end punctuation—periods, question marks, and exclamation marks.

## Punctuation That Ends All

*Consultant's recommendation:*
*When developing transcriptive formulations of functional activities intended as communicative vehicles for instructive documentation, it is incumbent upon the cognizant supervisory personnel to ensure that proper mechanical methodologies incorporating punctilious punctuation and grammatical rectification are surreptitiously employed.*

*Editor's note: Put a sock in it!*

Every sentence must end, but most do not end soon enough. Now is a good time to turn back to pages 94–96 and review run-on sentences and fragments. As a general rule, keep your punctuation simple by writing short sentences— five to twenty-two words is a good length. Beyond twenty-two words, a reader's attention level drops rapidly.

**End punctutation** officially terminates a sentence. Every sentence ends with one of three punctuation marks: a period (.), a question mark (?), or an exclamation mark (!).

### THE PERIOD (.)

A period is used to end a declarative sentence—a sentence that makes a statement.

When you say *no* you must mean it.

Walking a tightrope takes skill and concentration.

**NOTE:** Always place a period *inside* quotation marks.

Mark Twain said, ''When angry, count four; when very angry, swear.''

Use a period when a question is intended as a suggestion, and an answer is not required.

> Hester asked if he was all right.

> May we hear from you within two weeks.

Periods follow many abbreviations and contractions.

| | | |
|---|---|---|
| Washington, D.C. | Jr. | i.e. |
| Ms. | Dec. | etc. |
| e.g. | attn. | Dr. |
| p.m. | B.C. | Mon. |

HEADS UP:  Stop only once at the end of a sentence. Do not use a period *after* a quotation mark. When you use quotation marks, the period is always placed *inside* the final mark.

NOT:  William James once said, ''The art of being wise is the art of knowing what to overlook''.

YES:  William James once said, ''The art of being wise is the art of knowing what to overlook.''

## THE QUESTION MARK (?)

The question mark is used to end a sentence that asks a question.

> What are you doing in the wine cellar?

> Are you all right?

Place a question mark inside a direct quotation.

> Maggie whined, ''Why don't you come out of there?''

Sometimes question marks are placed in parentheses to indicate doubt or uncertainty.

> When it is not necessary to make a decision, it is necessary not to make a decision. *Lord Falkland (1610?–1643)*

> Suki said the books were out of balance by 80,000(?) dollars.

## THE EXCLAMATION MARK (!)

The exclamation mark (also called an exclamation point) is used as end punctuation to show strong emotion or surprise. It is used also to emphasize strong words or sentences, or to indicate a forceful command or request.
Use these marks sparingly. They seldom have a place in business writing. Do not use two exclamation marks for extra emphasis, because they look tacky and they weaken your point. See what I mean!!

Stop, you knave!

Get out of my face!

No! Your boa constrictor stays home.

''Bring me the Bloopers Report this instant!'' shouted Spiro.

## ■ EXERCISE FOR PRACTICE

Place the proper end punctuation mark (a period, a question mark, or an exclamation mark) at the end of each of the following sentences. Check your answers at the end of this section.

Examples:   Why are we meeting like this?

Wasting time is a useful part of life.

It's an earthquake! Get into a doorway!

1. Professor Wolfman requests that no one smoke in the lecture hall

2. We're in deep yogurt now

3. Give me a break

4. Isn't the scheduling report due on Friday

5. The best angle from which to approach a problem is the try-angle

6. Yes We've found the data

7. Did you see Bob get out of that empty cab

8. Be still my heart

# Don't Be A Comma-Kazi

> *When you have trouble getting commas right, chances are you're trying to patch up a poorly structured sentence.*
> —Claire Kehrwald Cook

The comma is a signal that tells readers to slow down, pause, and proceed. Commas are meant to make writing easier to read. Although some comma rules are as permanent as graffiti in granite, many are not; so use your "comma sense" to determine where you would pause naturally. Commas are important because they can change the meaning of your sentence—for better or worse.

In the water bugs look bigger.

In the water, bugs look bigger.

To Peggy Sue was shallow and superficial.

To Peggy, Sue was shallow and superficial.

The following comma rules have been approved by the Society for the Prevention of Punishment by Punctuation. These are the rules you need, although there are others—for the obsessively correct and punctuationally deranged.

## RULE ONE

Use commas to introduce words, phrases, and clauses. Introductory commas allow you to skim less important introductory information and focus on the main idea of the sentence.

### Words

Manuel, please submit your resume.

Yes, your way is best.

Incidentally, our first quarter earnings are up.

**A Danged Exception:**  Do not place a single comma after *but, and, so, yet* and so on, when you begin a sentence with one of these words. Be careful to use these words sparingly as first words in sentences, because they are not used often and they may distract or confuse your reader.

And the band played on.

But my ship never came in.

## Phrases

In conclusion, we appreciate your contribution to this worthwhile charity.

While waiting for the train, Zorba read *USA Today.*

Due to circumstances beyond my control, I've been promoted.

## Clauses

If you need additional information, please hesitate to call.

While you were out, morale improved.

**NOTE:** If you flip-flop the clauses in the three examples above, you do not need commas.

Please hesitate to call if you need additional information.

Morale improved while you were out.

Old age isn't so bad when you consider the alternative.

## ■ EXERCISE FOR PRACTICE

In the following sentences, insert the necessary commas after the introductory words, phrases, or clauses. Check your answers at the end of this section.

Examples:   Finally, we have decided not to decide.

Speaking off the record, we expect to double our profits next year.

As the crowd grew restless, the candidates made more promises.

1. If the phone rings let the answering machine get it.

2. On days that begin with morning Bainbreath picks up his messages and relaxes over coffee.

3. No we aren't going to solve this problem with a bulldozer.

4. During the two weeks before the election campaign headquarters was crowded with volunteers.

5. Because things aren't going as planned you can assume that we never had a plan.

6. Seriously we can only spend our budget once.

7. Although you possess many fine skills most of them were obsolete shortly after the Industrial Revolution.

8. By the way we found no problem to match your solution.

## RULE TWO

Use commas to separate items (words, phrases, and clauses) in a series. A series is three or more items. Some writers omit the comma before the final *and* or *or* in a series. However, this comma is always correct and it provides clarity for your readers. They will be pleased. The final comma *is* optional, and you do not have to use it if the meaning is clear without it.

WORDS:      Participants included accountants, bookkeepers, and the IRS.

PHRASES:    Herkimer sought his revenge by entering his boss' office, dialing the number of ''time'' in Japan, and leaving the phone off the hook over the weekend.

CLAUSES:    Hortense attended an aviator training school, she applied for a job with the airlines, and she became the first fly-by-night navigator in history.

## ■ EXERCISE FOR PRACTICE

In the following sentences, count the items. If a sentence contains three or more items in a series, use commas to separate them. The comma before the final *and* or *or* is optional; however, the answer key includes the final comma for clarity. Write OK next to those sentences that do not require commas. Check your answers at the end of this section.

Examples:   Philippa attended the early meeting and ate breakfast with the president. OK

Rory, Tyrone, and Earnest are leaving for Australia tonight.

Company sweatshirts are available in the cafeteria, at the reception desk, or in the employee relations office.

1. Management responsibility includes sending out surveys noting and initiating and taking issues under advisement.

2. The librarian purchased sixteen volumes of the *Oxford English Dictionary* and the *Encyclopedia Mathematica.*

3. Eat drink and be cheery.

4. After three days Elvira throws out newspapers friends and leftovers.

5. I would bet a month's salary my subscription to *Star Trek* magazine and the boss' stereo that my plan will work.

6. Can we bend the rules and submit our reports after the first of the month?

7. Your inquiry was sent to upper management their consultants and the finance committee for consideration.

8. Washing your clothes on the gentle cycle is much more humane.

**More danged exceptions:**

1. Do not use a comma with only two items.

    Pass the salt and pepper.

2. Do not use a comma when you use *and* or *or* between every item.

    Would you like Mondays or Tuesdays or Fridays off?

3. You do not need a comma in certain adjective-noun combinations when they are thought of as almost one word. In such cases, the adjective preceding the adjective-noun combination does not need a comma.

    a recreational <u>heart transplant</u>     the new <u>CD player</u>

    a regular <u>dog-and-pony show</u>     a real <u>one-man band</u>

## RULE THREE

Use a comma after the first of two independent clauses (a compound sentence) that are joined by these coordinating conjunctions: *and, but, or, nor, for, yet, so.*

    You can't win them all, but you sure can lose them all.

Remember that independent clauses are complete thoughts and they can stand alone. Do not use a comma before the coordinating conjunction if the clause on each side is not a complete thought. As a method of testing independent clauses, cover the word *but* in the example above. Notice that the clauses on both sides are independent and that they could stand alone as complete sentences. In the following sentence cover the word *and*.

Rhoda twitched nervously and bit her nails.

The first clause is independent, but *bit her nails* is not. Therefore, Rule Three does not apply to this sentence. (For a review of coordinating conjunctions, see page 60.)

## ■ EXERCISE FOR PRACTICE

Circle the coordinating conjunction in the following sentences. If the conjunction joins two complete thoughts, insert a comma before the conjunction.

Examples:   We appreciate your input, (but) we have enough unscientific data already.

Everyone (but) Fiorello completed the bungee jumping class successfully.

1. You and I need a vacation.

2. Everyone has ideas that don't work and I have mine.

3. Please don't resign for you are the only one who knows the system.

4. You must advise me so I will have someone to blame if the project fails.

5. Have you analyzed the data and the projections yet?

6. Put a small amount of money away each month and at the end of the year you'll be surprised at how little you have.

7. To err is human but to forgive is not our policy.

8. Phuong works three jobs yet she shows up on time with a cheerful smile.

**Alert! Alert!**

Now that you have completed this exercise, you may be interested to know that it is acceptable to drop the comma if a compound sentence is short, if the two clauses are closely related, and if the sentence is easy to understand without the comma. For example, in Sentence 2 of the previous exercise, you can drop the comma.

## RULE FOUR

Words or phrases that interrupt the flow of a sentence or are unnecessary for the main idea are set off by commas. Following are five examples of interrupting words and phrases.

### Parenthetical Words and Phrases

A **parenthetical expression** is a word or a phrase that is inserted into a sentence whose main thought would be complete without it.

> *As a matter of fact,* facts are seldom facts.

> My promotion was, *to put it mildly,* long overdue.

> *Generally speaking,* a desk is a wastebasket with drawers.

### Tag Questions

A **tag question** repeats the helping verb in a negative manner at the end of the sentence. In most cases the one asking the question already knows the answer.

> You are keeping my secret, *aren't you?*

> Rinalda is a magician, *isn't she?*

> You'll help with the project, *won't you?*

### Transitional Words and Phrases

Set off words and phrases such as *well, yes, no, oh, nevertheless, finally,* and so on, when they appear at the beginning of a sentence. These words seldom have any grammatical connection to the sentence. Transitional words are different from parenthetical expressions because parentheticals are seldom used to bridge from one sentence to the next. Transitional words create a flow from one idea to another, and from one sentence to the next.

> *Oh,* I didn't realize you were busy.

> *Nevertheless,* you will climb the ladder of success more easily if you lay it flat.

> *Finally,* we have a signed contract.

### Interjections

Set off mild exclamations that do not have a grammatical connection to the sentence.

*Hey,* get a grip.

*Oops,* I have the wrong number.

*Well now,* this is a fine mess you've gotten us into.

## Direct Address

Use a comma to set off the names of persons, places, or things being addressed.

*Paris,* here I come.

*Roland,* you need a breath mint.

*Hey,* you old so-and-so, I've missed you.

### ■ EXERCISE FOR PRACTICE

To practice working with interrupting material in sentences, insert commas wherever they are needed in the following sentences. Check your answers at the end of this section.

Examples:   It's possible, I realize, that my sole purpose in life is to serve as a warning to others.

Generally speaking, the temperature in the office is either too hot or too cold.

1. I believe a cluttered desk is the mark of a genius don't you?
2. Remember the best person you interview isn't necessarily the best person for the job.
3. The facts although interesting are irrelevant.
4. Yessiree it's better to be lucky than smart.
5. Of course if it's in stock we have it.
6. Worry they say kills more people than work ever will.
7. Everyone in the office was there weren't they?
8. Okay I'll think it over.

### RULE FIVE

**Nonrestrictive** elements (often introduced by the words *which* or *whose*) are parenthetical, meaning that the information they add is *not* vital to the meaning of the sentence. Set off nonrestrictive information with commas. **Restrictive** elements, on the other hand, are vital to the meaning of the sentence. Following is a short review of restrictive and nonrestrictive elements in a sentence. Steady now, here we go.

**Restrictive** elements are words, phrases, or clauses in a sentence that are essential to the meaning of the sentence. They identify the preceding noun and answer the question, "Which one?" You do not set off these elements with commas.

> The tickets *for the turkey raffle* are on your desk.

> (The phrase *for the turkey raffle* tells which tickets, so it is restrictive and is not set off by commas.)

> He *who hesitates* is bossed.

> (*Who hesitates* specifies which person, so the clause is restrictive and is not set off by commas.)

Uncertainty would rein if we left out the restrictive clauses in the sentences above. *The tickets are on your desk.* (Which tickets? To Outer Mundania? The World Series? Traffic school?) *He is bossed.* (What kind of a person is bossed? A henpecked husband? A nineties kind of guy? Anyone who works for someone else?)

**Nonrestrictive** elements add interesting details (even profound thought) to a sentence, but they are not vital to its meaning. Therefore, they are set off by commas. In the following examples the elements in italics are nonrestrictive. The sentences would be clear without them.

> Mee Tu, *who lives in my dorm,* is graduating in three years.

> (The clause, *who lives in my dorm,* isn't essential; without it we have: *Mee Tu is graduating in three years.*)

> My job, *which is marginally better than daytime TV,* pays my tuition and the rent.

> (Without the nonrestrictive clause *which is marginally better than daytime TV* we have: *My job pays my tuition and the rent.*)

Compare the following sentences.

> The blueprints *that I need* are on my desk. (essential)

> The blueprints, *which we completed yesterday,* are on my desk. (nonessential)

Differences between restrictive and nonrestrictive elements in a sentence won't always be obvious. You will have to think carefully about them, especially phrases and clauses beginning with *who, whose,* or *which.*

> The woman *who is coming down the hall* is my manager. (restrictive)

> The woman, *who happens to be my manager,* owns stock in Walmart. (nonrestrictive)

To make your job easier, try using *that* to introduce restrictive clauses and *which* to introduce nonrestrictive clauses.

> Ice cream *that is flavored with artificial sweeteners* is boring. (restrictive)

> Ice cream, *which is my weakness,* is a great pacifier. (nonrestrictive)

**NOTE:** Some editors go on ''which hunts'' in order to elminate nonrestrictive (nonessential) clauses. If they are nonessential, why include them? There is some wisdom here.

### ■ EXERCISE FOR PRACTICE

Insert commas around nonrestrictive elements in the following sentences. If a sentence is okay as it is, write **OK** next to it. Check your answers at the end of this section.

Examples:   Someone who keeps pet wallabies should have room for them to roam.

Belinda Boomerang, who keeps pet wallabies, sings soprano in the chorus.

1. Mr. Chisel a man who hates to spend money was nominated for several awards.

2. Those who arrived late missed the meeting.

3. Any parent whose child has ever taken drum lessons will admit that even suicide has its appealing moments.

4. Drusilla said that she got a headache whenever she tried to see things her boss' way.

5. Reginald one of the Regis twins has a blue eye and a green eye.

6. Vidalia who lives in Boston is riding her bicycle through England.

7. You should have seen the one that got away.

8. The road to Glory being paved with good intentions was closed for repairs.

## RULE SIX

Use one or more commas to set off direct quotes or quoted material from the rest of the sentence. Note that the comma goes inside the quotation marks in direct quotations.

"Never do anything for the first time," the swami murmured wisely.

"Since there's no special reason," said Bubba, "it must be government policy."

The helpful hardware man told my uncle, "The leak in the roof is never in the same location as the drip."

Lucas glared at his fiancée, pouted his lip, and said, "If you cared more about my feelings, you wouldn't be so successful."

Be careful not to set off indirect quotes with commas.

My father always said it was easier to make money than it was to earn a living.

I was told that no job is too small to screw up.

## ■ EXERCISE FOR PRACTICE

In the following sentences, insert commas where they are needed to set off direct quotes from the rest of the sentence. Check your answers at the end of this section.

Examples:   "I can't have a crisis next week," stated Henry, "because my calendar is full."

"Will the last one off the planet please turn off the lights," said Irma dryly.

1. "Please open your blue books and begin the test" stated the instructor.
2. James Thurber said "It is better to know some of the questions than all of the answers."
3. "Where I am in my career today" said Barbara "has everything to do with hanging on by my fingernails."
4. "Let's build a fire and study for our exam" said Adlai.
5. "As for you, Fido" said Jess sternly "you're in deep yogurt."
6. "I really appreciate you" smiled Lee Chan.

7. "And I" Ruprecht replied "really appreciate you."

8. Ashleigh sighed "I resent being treated like the sort of person I really am."

## What, More Comma Rules? Yes, a Few.

### RULE SEVEN

Use a comma in place of omitted words.

> Bea Gohn works for Apple Computer; her husband, for IBM.

> I'll move to New Mexico; you, to New Guinea.

### RULE EIGHT

Use a comma after a greeting in a personal letter, and after the complimentary closing in all letters.

> Dear Samantha,

> All the best,

**NOTE:** Use a colon after the salutation of a business letter.

> Dear Mr. Datameister:

### RULE NINE

Use a comma in dates and addresses. Put commas before and after the year when a date is written in month-day-year order.

> Your letter of April 1, 1993, has been forwarded to our order department.

> On May 29, 1942, I was born in Reno, Nevada, during a late spring snow storm.

If the date is written in day-month-year order, omit the commas.

> Your letter of 1 April 1993 has been forwarded to me.

Place a comma between the city and state in addresses. Do not place a comma between the state and the zip code.

> Justin Doit

> 111 Nike Blvd.

> Menlo Park, CA 00000

## RULE TEN

Use a comma to prevent misunderstanding.

> If you ask Bob will run the meeting.
>
> If you ask, Bob will run the meeting.

> Once Denzel understood the reason was clear.
>
> Once Denzel understood, the reason was clear.

> Outside the wolves howled.
>
> Outside, the wolves howled.

## RULE ELEVEN

Set off an appositive with commas. **Appositives** are words or phrases that rename a preceding noun.

> My ex-roommate, Sam, is now a big-time banking executive.
>
> The hermit crab, a grouchy fellow, seals himself inside his shell for life.

## ■ EXERCISE FOR PRACTICE

The following sentences review Rules Seven through Eleven. Insert commas where they are needed in each of the following sentences. Check your answers at the end of this section.

Examples:   Dear Angelo,

How good it was to hear from you.

Glen attends biology lab twice a week; English class, once.

1. Dear Edgar Your case for an afterlife is most convincing.
2. My favorite movie star Robin Williams is a talented comedian.
3. To begin with new computers are expensive.
4. Running the bulls broke into the plaza.
5. Men are from Mars; women from Venus.
6. Elvin arrived in Bangkok Thailand on Monday June 1 1993.

7. Please write when you can. Sincerely Michael

8. The Zoo Hour

   KGO Radio

   900 Front Street

   San Francisco CA 00000

## A FINAL WORD ABOUT COMMAS:

After studying commas, you may be tempted to overpunctuate your sentences. Resist. Fight the urge. Back off. Develop the habit of asking why you are using each comma. If you do not have a good reason and a rule to support it, leave out the comma. You'll be a better person for it.

# Are You Semiconscious About Semicolons?

> *Leaving out a semicolon when it is needed is like winking at someone in the dark; you know what you are doing, but no one else does.*

Most people are unsure of semicolons. Actually, the rules for their use are few and simple. Here are the ones you should know.

## RULE ONE

A semicolon (;) is like an industrial-strength comma, but it is weaker than a period. Many semicolons in a document mean that the writing is formal, or that the writer is confused. A semicolon is used most frequently to join two independent clauses when you do not use a connecting word (*and, but, or, nor, for, yet, so*).

   You are wild and unstable; I like that in a person.

   The number of mergers is up; the number of investors is down.

A semicolon provides balance in writing; however, you should not overuse it. Commas can be used to join independent clauses as well, or you can write two sentences. Writers often wish they did not have so many choices, yet each punctuation mark gives the sentence a slightly different meaning.

I was pleased to answer promptly; I said I did not know.

Although I was pleased to answer promptly, I said I did not know.

I answered promptly. I said I did not know.

*Paraphrased from Mark Twain*

## RULE TWO

In compound sentences a semicolon precedes the following connecting words called **conjunctive adverbs**. Some conjunctive adverbs that you may recognize include the following:

| | | |
|---|---|---|
| accordingly | instead | still |
| besides | likewise | then |
| hence | moreover | therefore |
| however | nevertheless | thus |
| indeed | otherwise | |

You must take six science courses this semester; otherwise you will not graduate.

Klinger was not fired with enthusiasm; therefore, he was fired with enthusiasm.

**NOTE:** The comma after some conjunctive adverbs is optional. You will be correct if you follow the conjunctive adverb with a comma; however, you can leave it out if the sentence is short and clear without it.

Our inventory is low; nevertheless we plan to continue with one shift.

Everything Ms. Wannabe says is politically correct; however, I question her motives.

## RULE THREE

Use a semicolon between items in a series when the items already contain commas.

The referee ejected Refrigerator Washington, the nose tackle; Weezle Traction, the left guard; and Roman Jones, the line coach, from the game.

**NOTE:** The semicolon is placed outside quotation marks and parentheses.

Ignorance is not ''bliss''; it is exile.

Wihelm has lots of money (he got it the really old-fashioned way); he inherited it.

■ **EXERCISE FOR PRACTICE**

Punctuate the following sentences using semicolons as needed. Check your answers at the end of this section.

Examples:   As Mark Twain said, ''The rain will stop; it always does.''

Time is short; therefore, we wish to negotiate the contract immediately.

1. I want to review the performance evaluation for Tad Frumpy however I wish for this matter to remain our little secret.

2. Miss Georgia Peach has such a positive attitude she suffers from terminal optimism.

3. Every successful person has suffered failures but repeated failure is no guarantee of eventual success.

4. We plan to build new facilities in Bangor Maine Pierre South Dakota Fort Scott Kansas and Texarkana Texas.

5. Our standards for employment are high we require that you wear shoes and a shirt and you must be able to dance the lambada.

6. Please take a seat fill out the form and enjoy our complimentary copy of *War and Peace* the doctor will be with you shortly.

7. The branch office is not reporting regularly however they have always shown a profit.

8. Sterling has one unmatched asset he can yawn with his mouth closed in our staff meetings.

# Uppercase—A Capital Idea

*Speaking and writing without your audience in mind is like writing a love letter and addressing it to: To Whom It May Concern.*

Capitalization is a writer's tool that focuses special attention on certain words by writing the first letter of the word in uppercase type; for example, Washington, D.C. To make your decisions about capitalizing easier, follow this important rule: **Always have a specific reason for capitalizing a word.** Some capitalization rules are easy; they are standard guidelines you can count on. You will find them listed below with examples of each. However, you will probably hear many different opinions about what should and should not be capitalized. When writers aren't sure of the rules, they are likely to capitalize words randomly for any of the following reasons:

1. To uphold established traditions of capitalization within their organizations

2. To show respect for authority

3. To play it safe when they are uncertain about the rules

4. To emphasize key words

Be smart here. You are far better off knowing the rules than guessing at them. It's a no-no to make them up as you go. Take time to read through this section, then keep this book close by and refer to it until you are sure of the most common uses of capital letters.

In general, capitalize the first letter of all proper nouns, the first letter of the first word of a sentence, and the first letter of the first word in a direct quotation. The purpose of capital letters is to help your reader by making your meaning clear.

**NOTE:** A current dictionary is still the best reference for correct capitalization.

### RULE ONE

Capitalize proper nouns and adjectives made from proper nouns. A proper noun is a specific person, place, or thing. A proper adjective is formed from a proper noun: Europe (proper noun); European (proper adjective).

| Proper Noun | Common Noun |
|---|---|
| Garfield | comic strip character |
| Arkansas | state |
| Monday | long day |
| University of Texas | school |
| the International Listening Association | organization |

In general, a name that accompanies a capitalized word is also capitalized if it is a part of the specific name. If it stands alone, it is not capitalized.

| | |
|---|---|
| Senator Feinstein | the senator from California |
| Golden Gate Park | a park in San Francisco |
| Washington State | the state of Washington |
| President Clinton | the president of the United States |
| Tropic of Cancer | the tropics |
| Webster's Dictionary | a dictionary by Webster |
| Christmas Eve | the night before Christmas |
| Beverly Hills High School | a high school in Beverly Hills |

**A.** Capitalize specific persons, tribes, races, nationalities, and languages.

| | | |
|---|---|---|
| Alice Cooper | Greek | French |
| Asian | Apache | Bill Clinton |

**NOTE:** Racial descriptions such as black and white are not usually capitalized; however, check your dictionary. For instance, a native Californian is a person born in that state; a Native American is an American Indian.

**B.** Capitalize specific places: geographical locations, countries, cities, states; rivers, oceans, and seas; parks, monuments, buildings, rooms, and so forth.

| | | |
|---|---|---|
| Germany | Norfolk | Columbia River |
| New Hampshire | Yosemite National Park | the Red Sea |
| Indian Ocean | Crater Lake | Laurel Street |
| Eiffel Tower | Vietnam Memorial | Room 54 |

**C.** Capitalize astronomical bodies.

| | | |
|---|---|---|
| the Big Dipper | the Horeshead nebula | Halley's comet |
| Jupiter | Betelgeuse (Beetlejuice) | Ursa Major |

**NOTE:** The earth, moon, and sun are not capitalized unless they are used with other astronomical terms that are capitalized.

**D.** Capitalize names of deities.

| | | |
|---|---|---|
| God | the Virgin Mary | Jehovah |
| Allah | Buddha | Diana |

**E.** Capitalize historical periods, events, and documents.

| | | |
|---|---|---|
| North American Trade Agreement | | Dark Ages |
| World War II | Russian Revolution | Great Depression |
| the Me Decade | Age of Enlightenment | Boston Tea Party |

**F.** Capitalize specific organizations, associations, and institutions.

| | | |
|---|---|---|
| Oakland Athletics | Hertz Rental Cars | McDonald's |
| Sierra Club | Red Cross | Catholic Church |
| Smithsonian Institute | London Philharmonic | Coca-Cola Company |

**G.** Capitalize the days of the week, months, and holidays.

| | | |
|---|---|---|
| Thursday | May | Easter |

**H.** Capitalize government and judicial groups.

| | |
|---|---|
| United Nations | U.S. Senate |
| European Economic Community | Municipal Court of Miami |
| Parliament | Supreme Court |

**I.** Capitalize ships, aircraft, spacecraft, and trains.

| | | |
|---|---|---|
| the Love Boat | Concorde | Orient Express |
| Goodyear Blimp | Starship Enterprise | Voyager IX |

**J.** Capitalize initials showing time, governmental departments, call letters for radio and TV stations, and other well-known sets of initials.

| | | | | |
|---|---|---|---|---|
| CIA | A.D. | TV | NASA | PPC |
| CD | RAM | IBM | NASDAC | 1-800-DENTIST |

**K.** Capitalize points of the compass that refer to a specific geographic location. Also capitalize regions when they are specific sections or parts of a precise descriptive title.

> the Western Hemisphere      New York's East Side      the South

Do not capitalize general directions.

> east of St. Louis                    southern Indiana
>
> west of the mountains          northern states
>
> a south-central location       western slopes

**L.** Use capital letters for the first word of every sentence, including sentence fragments, words and phrases used as sentences, and quoted material.

> When will this project be finished? Never!
>
> Of course. Why? O.K. Beats me.
>
> Ms. Pettibone Poole states, ''He who laughs, lasts.''

Do not capitalize the first words of:

> *An indirect quotation:* My manager said that she was pleased with the Seifert report.
>
> *A phrase set off with quotes:* Words are the most potent ''drug of choice'' used by human beings.

**M.** Use capital letters for the first word of a formal statement or a question following a colon.

> The interviewer asked these questions: What are your goals? What are your skills? Why are you applying here?
>
> Here is my best advice: Do your work the best way that you can, and be kind.

**N.** Capitalize the most important words in titles, including the first and last words. Do not capitalize conjunctions (*and, or, but*) articles (*a, and, the*), and short prepositions (*for, by, in, at, to,* and so forth). Always capitalize the verbs in titles.

> *Megatrends for Women (book)*
>
> ''Ode to Joy'' *(choral work)*

Symphony No. 9 *(classical music)*

''The Croissantization of America'' *(article)*

''How to Find Joy in the Dictionary'' *(chapter)*

**O.** Capitalize the first and last words in the salutation (greeting) of a letter and the first word in the complimentary close.

Dear Sir: *(salutation)*

My winsome little Chickadee, *(salutation)*

Very truly yours, *(complimentary close)*

Sincerely, *(complimentary close)*

**P.** Capitalize the first word in each line of poetry, even if a new line begins in the middle of a sentence.

I must go down to the seas again,

To the lonely sea and sky,

And all I ask is a tall ship

And a star to steer her by;

''Sea Fever'' *by John Masefield*

**NOTE:** Many modern poets ignore this rule, thus the term ''poetic license.'' Some poets such as e.e. cummings use no capitalization whatsoever.

## WHEN NOT TO CAPITALIZE WORDS

1. Do not capitalize the names of animals, birds, trees, foods, games, diseases, or seasons, unless they contain proper nouns. Capitalize the seasons if they are personified.

| | | | |
|---|---|---|---|
| mongoose | English sparrow | box elder | pizza |
| French wine | hide and seek | measles | winter |
| Lyme disease | Old Man Winter | California live oak | Monopoly |

2. Do not capitalize *a, an,* or *the* before a title or name unless they are a part of the title or name.

the *National Inquirer*      the *New York Times*

the Honorable Judge Wapner      *The Shining*

3. Do not capitalize words that denote family relationships, when they follow a possessive noun or pronoun.

> Clara is my aunt from Montreal.
>
> Sean's mother is visiting from Ireland.
>
> Moppie's sister and brother own stock in the company.

*Do* capitalize family relationships when used as a title preceding a name, or by itself as if it were a name.

> Aunt Clara is from Montreal.
>
> Where are the cookies, Mom?
>
> Sisters and Brothers, we have a great challenge ahead.

4. Do not capitalize school subjects unless they are languages, titles of specific classes, or proper names.

> mathematics       Spanish              Differential Calculus II
>
> biology           foreign languages    Ancient Egyptian History

5. Do not capitalize school names, classes, or semesters, unless they are proper nouns.

> Beginning second semester, Franco will be a junior in college.
>
> Franco is president of the Sophomore Class at Illinois University.

6. Do not capitalize just any old word you want to emphasize. (Use italics or underlining instead.)

> WRONG:   Do NOT break the glass.
>
> RIGHT:   Do *not* break the glass.
>
> RIGHT:   Do <u>not</u> break the glass.

7. Do not capitalize the second part of most compound words, unless the second part is a proper noun.

> Fifty-fourth Avenue                    all-American
>
> anti-matter                            pro-British

■ **EXERCISE FOR PRACTICE**

Proofread the following sentences, and capitalize according to the rules you have just studied. Check your answers at the end of this section.

Examples:  *I* don't think *K*arl is clear on the concept of the chaos theory.

*P*lease send the *J*ones report to *E*lmo *B*eezer, 221 *f* street, *$t. *l*ouis, *m*issouri, 00000.

1. the senator from idaho will be at memorial stadium on august 2.

2. we are taking a dc-10 to dover, delaware, on wednesday morning.

3. i am a great believer in luck, and i find the harder i work the more i have of it.—stephen leacock, quoted by robert w. kent, *money talks*, 1985. ''entrepreneurs''

4. ''designer genes'' are genetic materials that have been altered through scientific engineering for use in agriculture and medicine.

5. the entire western hemisphere will be affected by the north american trade agreement.

6. my colleague is reading *how to make a million in the nineties*.

■ **EXERCISE FOR PRACTICE**

In the following sentence change incorrectly capitalized words to lowercase. Check your answers at the end of this section.

Examples:  A *m*eeting is no substitute for *p*rogress.

Never eat in a *r*estaurant named Mom's, play *p*oker with a man

named Doc, or buy a *f*oreign car from someone named Frenchy.

1. PLEASE do not disturb.

2. Our Department reports to the Company Treasurer and the Engineering Manager at the Westside Office.

3. The Summer Meeting of The Insurance Underwriters Of America will be held in Scottsdale, Arizona, on the Western Slope of Saddleback Mountain.

4. The Democratic Party will hold its Annual Convention during the Spring Break.

5. Apathy is a Major Problem in our Organization—BUT WHO CARES?

# Answers for Section IV

## PUNCTUATION

Page 131

1. Period (.)
2. Exclamation mark (!)
3. Question mark (?)
4. Comma (,)
5. Semicolon (;)
6. Colon (:)

7. Dash (—)
8. Parenthesis ( )
9. Apostrophe (')
10. Hyphen (-)
11. Quotation marks (" ")
12. Elipses (...)

## END PUNCTUATION

Page 134

1. Professor Wolfman requests that no one smoke in the lecture hall.
2. We're in deep yogurt now. OR We're in deep yogurt now!
3. Give me a break!
4. Isn't the scheduling report due on Friday?
5. The best angle from which to approach a problem is the try-angle.
6. Yes! We've found the data. OR We've found the data!
7. Did you see Bob get out of that empty cab?
8. Be still my heart. OR Be still my heart!

## COMMAS

Page 136

1. If the phone rings, let the answering machine get it.
2. On days that begin with morning, Bainbreath picks up his messages and relaxes over coffee.

3. No, we aren't going to solve this problem with a bulldozer.

4. During the two weeks before the election, campaign headquarters was crowded with volunteers.

5. Because things aren't going as planned, you can assume that we never had a plan.

6. Seriously, we can only spend our budget once.

7. Although you possess many fine skills, most of them were obsolete shortly after the Industrial Revolution.

8. By the way, we found no problem to match your solution.

## COMMAS

Page 137

1. Management responsibility includes sending out surveys, noting and initiating, and taking issues under advisement.

2. The librarian purchased sixteen volumes of the *Oxford English Dictionary* and the *Encyclopedia Mathematica*. OK

3. Eat, drink, and be cheery.

4. After three days Elvira throws out newspapers, friends, and leftovers.

5. I would bet a month's salary, my subscription to *Star Trek* magazine, and the boss' stereo that my plan will work.

6. Can we bend the rules and submit our reports after the first of the month? OK

7. Your inquiry was sent to upper management, their consultants, and the finance committee for consideration.

8. Washing your clothes on the gentle cycle is much more humane. OK

## COMMAS AND COORDINATING CONJUNCTIONS

Page 139

1. You (and) I need a vacation.

2. Everyone has ideas that don't work, (and) I have mine.

3. Please don't resign, (for) you are the only one who knows the system.

4. You must advise me, (so) I will have someone to blame if the project fails.

5. Have you analyzed the data (and) the projections yet?

6. Put a small amount of money away each month, (and) at the end of the year you'll be surprised at how little you have.

7. To err is human, (but) to forgive is not our policy.

8. Phuong works three jobs, (yet) she shows up on time with a cheerful smile.

## COMMAS

Page 141

1. I believe a cluttered desk is the mark of a genius, don't you?

2. Remember, the best person you interview isn't necessarily the best person for the job.

3. The facts, although interesting, are irrelevant.

4. Yessiree, it's better to be lucky than smart.

5. Of course, if it's in stock we have it.

6. Worry, they say, kills more people than work ever will.

7. Everyone in the office was there, weren't they?

8. Okay, I'll think it over.

## COMMAS IN RESTRICTIVE AND NONRESTRICTIVE ELEMENTS

Pages 143

1. Mr. Chisel, a man who hates to spend money, was nominated for several awards.

2. Those who arrived late missed the meeting. OK

3. Any parent whose child has ever taken drum lessons will admit that even suicide has its appealing moments. OK

4. Drusilla said that she got a headache whenever she tried to see things her boss' way. OK

5. Reginald, one of the Regis twins, has a blue eye and a green eye.

6. Vidalia, who lives in Boston, is riding her bicycle through England.

7. You should have seen the one that got away. OK

8. The road to Glory, being paved with good intentions, was closed for repairs.

## COMMAS AND DIRECT QUOTATIONS

Page 144

1. ''Please open your blue books and begin the test,'' stated the instructor.

2. James Thurber said, ''It is better to know some of the questions than all of the answers.''

3. ''Where I am in my career today,'' said Barbara, ''has everything to do with hanging on by my fingernails.''

4. ''Let's build a fire and study for our exam,'' said Adlai.

5. ''As for you, Fido,'' said Jess sternly, ''you're in deep yogurt.''

6. ''I really appreciate you,'' smiled Lee Chan.

7. ''And I,'' Ruprecht replied, ''really appreciate you.''

8. Ashleigh sighed, ''I resent being treated like the sort of person I really am.''

## COMMAS FOR RULES SEVEN-ELEVEN

Page 146

1. Dear Edgar, Your case for an afterlife is most convincing.

2. My favorite movie star, Robin Williams, is a talented comedian.

3. To begin with, new computers are expensive.

4. Running, the bulls broke into the plaza.

5. Men are from Mars; women, from Venus.

6. Elvin arrived in Bangkok, Thailand, on Monday, June 1, 1993.

7. Please write when you can. Sincerely, Michael

8. The Zoo Hour

   KGO Radio

   900 Front Street

   San Francisco, CA 00000

## SEMICOLONS

Page 149

1. I want to review the performance evaluation for Tad Frumpy; however, I wish for this matter to remain our little secret.

2. Miss Georgia Peach has such a positive attitude; she suffers from terminal optimism.

3. Every successful person has suffered failures, but repeated failure is no guarantee of eventual success.

4. We plan to build new facilities in Bangor, Maine; Pierre, South Dakota; Fort Scott, Kansas; and Texarkana, Texas.

5. Our standards for employment are high; we require that you wear shoes and a shirt, and you must be able to dance the lambada.

6. Please take a seat, fill out the form, and enjoy our complimentary copy of *War and Peace*; the doctor will be with you shortly.

7. The branch office is not reporting regularly; however, they have always shown a profit.

8. Sterling has one unmatched asset; he can yawn with his mouth closed in our staff meetings.

## CAPITALIZATION

Page 156

1. The senator from Idaho will be at Memorial Stadium on August 2.

2. We are taking a DC-10 to Dover, Delaware, on Wednesday morning.

3. I am a great believer in luck, and I find the harder I work the more I have of it.—Stephen Leacock, quoted by Robert W. Kent, Money Talks, 1985. ''Entrepreneurs''

4. ''Designer genes'' are genetic materials that have been altered through scientific engineering for use in agriculture and medicine.

5. The entire Western Hemisphere will be affected by the North American Trade Agreement.

6. My colleague is reading *How to Make a Million in the Nineties*.

## CAPITALIZATION

Page 156–157

1. *Please* do not disturb.

2. Our department reports to the company treasurer and the engineering manager at the Westside office.

3. The summer meeting of the Insurance Underwriters of America will be held in Scottsdale, Arizona, on the western slope of Saddleback Mountain.

4. The Democratic Party will hold its annual convention during the spring break.

5. Apathy is a major problem in our organization—but who cares?

# Chapter V

# Communicating With Confidence

# Communicating With Confidence

> *The parade will take place in the morning if it rains in the afternoon.*
> —Sign posted on a Geneva street

Now that you have completed your learning, here are some useful tips for putting your new language skills into practice. When you speak or write, you should be direct and relevant. Respect your listener and your reader. Effective speakers and writers are interesting and they use simple language. Unless you are a true genius, settle for being clear. The following tips will help you to present your message skillfully when speaking and writing. When you use these guidelines, your receiver will appreciate your intelligence and professionalism.

## YOUR WORDS

- Be kind. *"I don't care what you know until I know you care."*
- Keep it simple.
- Put yourself in your receiver's place.
- Take responsibility for what you write and say.

## YOUR MESSAGE

- When speaking, look people in the eye.
- Tell your receiver what you want or need.
- Speak *to*, rather than *at* your receiver.
- Use preliminary tuning. *"Here is my point of view. Let me tell you why I feel that way."*
- Time your message. Wait for the right moment.

## YOUR ORGANIZATION

- State your main idea clearly and say it at the beginning of your message.
- Reinforce key points with repetition.
- Develop a logical sequence of information.
- Use little stories to illustrate your points.

## YOUR CLARITY

- Make every word pay its own way.
- Paint clear word pictures using visual nouns and vigorous verbs.
- Use appropriate transitions to connect your thoughts.
- Pause to allow time for the receiver to absorb your information.
- Use complete sentences, especially in writing.
- Pay attention to voice inflection and nonverbal communication.

## YOUR LANGUAGE

- Avoid lazy language—idioms, cliches, jargon, and exhausted expressions.
- Avoid all sexist language or inferences.
- Choose precise words and pronounce them accurately.
- Learn new words to increase your vocabulary.
- Use positive language.
- Think before you write or speak.

# Developing A Personal Action Plan

> *The reason many people never reach their goals is because they never set them.*
>
> —Unknown.

A definition of *accountability* is ''responsibility for one's actions.''

We all have good intentions. The thing that separates those who are successful from those who are not is how well these good intentions are carried out.

A voluntary action plan can convert your good intentions into actions.

The **personal action plan** on the next page is a good starting point if you are serious about improving your grammar and usage skills.

You can act on your plan any time you are reading, speaking, or listening (which is most of the time).

# Personal Action Plan

> *Decision making isn't a matter of arriving at a right or wrong answer, it's a matter of selecting the most effective course of action from less effective courses of action.*
>
> —Philip Marvin

Think about the information you have read in this book. Review the exercises. What did you learn about grammar and usage? What did you learn about your skills? How can you improve your ability to use English effectively? Make a commitment to improving your grammar and usage in your business and personal life. Design a personal action plan to help you reach your goal.

The following guide will help you clarify your goals and outline actions to achieve them.

1. My current grammar and usage skills are effective in the following areas:

2. I need to improve my grammar and usage skills in the following areas:

3. I will implement an action plan for improvement in the following manner:

    A. My goals for building my grammar and usage skills (be specific):

        Parts of speech:

        Writing complete sentences:

Using words effectively:

Improving spelling:

Punctuating correctly:

B.  My plan for reaching my goals:

C.  My timetable:

4.  The following people will benefit from my improved grammar and usage skills:

5.  They will benefit in the following ways: